WET

WET KNICKERS

Roy 'Chubby' Brown

ARROW BOOKS

Arrow Books Limited
62–65 Chandos Place, London WC2N 4NW

An imprint of Century Hutchinson Ltd

London Melbourne Sydney Auckland
Johannesburg and agencies throughout
the world

First published by Arrow 1986

© Roy Brown 1986

Illustrations © David English 1986

Printed and bound in Great Britain by
Anchor Brendon Limited, Tiptree, Essex

ISBN 0 09 946490 X

Contents

Chubby's Story

Me mam called me Roy after Roy Rogers – mind you, it was forty years after Roy Rogers. Dad was an electrician – excuse the pun, I was his first shock. I have an Uncle Bill who was a Methodist minister, my Auntie Connie is a lay preacher, so I must have been like a bone at a cat's wedding, something out of place.

I was born in the usual terraced house, the bog at the end of the yard with a big wooden seat which camouflaged the crabs. Those were the days of rock 'n' roll; it's all cock and dole now. My mother would economize by making me wear dad's cast-offs. His trousers gave me the most trouble, undoing the zip just to below me nose, but if you saw the size of me now you would swear I'd swallowed Cyril Smith. Talk about where I lived being a depression area – the woman next door threw herself out of the window. Good job it was a bungalow!

My first recollection was all the neighbours congregated round saying, 'Well, who would take her purse?' I bought £2 worth of broken biscuits with that money. Dad found out and took the skin off my arse. That's the one and only time I've ever lost weight. Houdini would never have got out of one of dad's headlocks. Dad would say, 'Stop talking to yourself or they'll lock you away.' That's his favourite saying.

I had a mate called Nander. By he was a tough kid: he used to bite the police dog. My mother and father fought like cat and dog, and eventually they got a divorce; I was about ten years old at the time. Material things we never

7

really had. Divorce wasn't fashionable then, either. Dad always used to say coming home to a cuddle meant you were in the wrong house. Dad and I lived alone for years. We were never really poor and never really rich. I mean, I never had to ring the NSPCC and say 'look Dad bought me a diamond watch and one of the stones was missing'.

I was like an Irish Robin Hood: I used to rob anybody and keep it. It was about that time that I saw my first hairy pussy. I soon fell in love with that – there was no way I was going to be a puff. Once I got the bug most of my pocket money went on dirty books. *Spic & Span*, it was called, that was my favourite. I used to think one day I'll be lucky enough to be on page 2 because page 3 had a massive pair of tits on it, and sooner or later somebody would come along and close the book and I would get them in my face.

I fucking hated school, didn't like the milk which you had to drink every morning at 10.00. Never forget taking a letter home to dad that said school meals are definitely going up, thinking to myself, 'Fucking hell, it takes me all my time to keep them down.'

I was an early Teddy Boy. I couldn't grow sideboards, so I used my sister's mascara pencil and drew them on. The trousers were that tight I had to grease my legs to get into them. I said to a friend one day, 'How do you manage to get that DA (short for duck's arse) in the back of your hair?' He said, 'I use lard.' The next night we went to a dance at the local hall. I'll never forget because Gerry & The Pacemakers, Billy J. Kramer and Marty Wilde were appearing there. My mate said, 'Roy, your fucking hair stinks.' Then proceeded to pull a piece of onion from behind my ear. He pissed himself laughing. You see, I'd took the lard from our frying pan after me mam had made the tea.

My other pal's name was Fuzzy. He'd always bring his sister round who was a few years older than me. She had – you've guessed it – great big tits, and used to let me feel them. On day Fuzzy broke into our gas meter. When me dad came home he blamed me, and I couldn't sit down for a week. He made me tell the police who had been round our house, which didn't matter anyway as they caught Fuzzy buying a Teddy Boy jacket with £15 of pennies. A daft cunt he was.

I was fifteen years old when I was picked for Grangetown Boys Cricket Team which is in Redcar. On the day of the match I ate what I thought was a bar of chocolate, but when I went in to bat I felt something running down my leg. I asked the captain if I could come off the pitch, yes he said, so I went to the toilet and I couldn't stop shitting. Some fucking chocolate that was, it was a full bar of laxatives. I was never off the bog for a week. Strange an athlete is what I've always wanted to be, in fact I've one of their feet.

Eventually the love of my life became music. I started playing the bass drum for North Ormsby Brass Band, and the highlight was the day Middlesbrough played Birmingham. We marched up and down the pitch, until some of the band went left and right. Not me – I couldn't see over the top of the drum and I walked into the fucking goalpost. After that I started playing the drums in the Station Hotel in Redcar. The piano player was a woman called Nancy Pinkley. She drank about eight pints of Guinness a night, and she'd fart so loud people thought that I'd put an extra beat on the bass drum. What a rough place it was, every Saturday night, but Nancy was too pissed to notice. Some nights I had to tell her the piano lid was still down. My drum kit was always being used as a weapon – I would have fought back but those days my legs were on a coward's body.

It was about that time I saw my first comic, a chap called Johnny Hammond, a very funny man. His cheeky grin and his warm approach made me love him to death. I thought, I wish I could do that, never thinking that we'd finish up being firm friends. After that it was a comic's life for me. My first line I can remember was: A traffic warden said, 'You can't park there, fatty,' and I said, 'I'm looking for a shit house.' The reply was 'You've found one.' Or:

Bought the wife a crocodile purse and it bit her wrist off. Or: They call my girlfriend Hokey Pokey. She puts it in, pulls it out, and shakes it about. The jokes were so pathetic they would have made rhubarb grow.

I decided to join the Navy, and still have a scar on my left arm which is six inches long. One of my fellow seamen tried to get my drawers off. I said 'fuck off' so he stabbed me. Those were the days – and seamen always say it's only rumours. Like fuck it is.

The jobs I've had are numerous: hod carrier, fitters' mate, painter, I once sold tickets at Blackpool's Pleasure Beach, I drove a wagon and a bus for ICI. One thing I've always had is a good memory. With my two cousins Derek and Lee Vasey we formed a pop group calling ourselves Pipe Line, but it didn't last long. Because of my memory I concentrated more on being a comic, buying books, records and tapes. Apart from that I had no option because I had my drums repossessed by the finance company. I tried all the talent competitions, auditions for 'Opportunity Knocks', 'New Faces', etc., never got anywhere, though. Them days my only claim to fame was that John Lennon once asked where he could get a cup of tea. However, that's another story. . . .

Bloody hell, did I starve in those days being a clean comic!

Wet Knickers

I went into a club one night and there was this bloody big fat woman – you know the type. She was so fat wherever she sat in the room she was next to you. She was standing at the bar, and I walked up to her, thinking I'd buy her a drink. I said, 'Bloody Mary?' She said, 'No, it's frigging Doris actually.' I said, 'Has anybody ever told you you're beautiful?' She said, 'No.' I said, 'I'm not surprised.' I asked her if she'd like to dance, and she said, 'No, thanks.' I said, 'I suppose a wank's out of the question, is it?'

●

Well, I'm not saying she was a tart, but she had a mattress tied to her back. I said, 'What's your name?' She said, 'Well, me boyfriend calls me Marge, 'cause me legs spread easily.' Eggs 50p a dozen down there. She'd swallowed more seamen than the Bermuda Triangle.

I took her to the cinema the next evening. The film was so old, James Bond drove a Ford Popular. She said, 'Chubby, we've only been in this cinema ten minutes and you've put your hands down me knickers twice.' I said, 'Come off it, love, only once.' She said, 'Well you're not going, are you?' She smelled like a London postman's socks on Giro day. She stunk so bad that when she threatened to commit suicide I told her to shoot herself in the armpit.

I might be fat but I've got a willie like a blind cobbler's thumb. You should have seen Marge up the back alley after ten minutes. Her face was a picture, and she was

11

moaning loudly. I said, 'Am I hurting you?' She said, 'No, you're standing on me fucking toe.'

•

I'm so unlucky. I found a wage packet, and the bastard had had three days off. If I'd been on the *Titanic* it would have fallen off its rafters in dry dock. I once had a bet on a horse and the jockey got off halfway round the track and asked the nightwatchman what horse won the race.

•

I only get women because of what I am – a racist. Now don't blame me. I got my sex education watching the dogs in our street. For years I went around smelling women's arses.

•

My wife went off me. I told her she'd changed her bloody tune. She said, 'Well, what about Friday – we're making love on the couch and your bloody daft mate come to the door and you just got up, no regard for me at all, and went straight to the door. I said, 'I had to go to the door.' She replied, 'There was no need to take me with you.'

That night in bed she got really annoyed with me. 'You've just got no manners at all,' she complained. 'When we go for a meal in a restaurant you use your manners at the table, don't you?' I said, 'Excuse me darling, pass the fanny.'

•

My wife told me her friend Margaret charged her husband £2 every time he has his leg over and she'd got loads of clothes. 'Why don't we try that from now on?' But she must have been feeling randy because when I said I was skint she said, 'I'll lend you a couple of quid until Thursday.'

•

Well, it's funny, ya know, but you women have a little place. You only have to touch it, 'aven't ya, and the legs are at 20 to 4, aren't they?

●

They say marriage is an institution – who the hell wants to live in an institution? Do you know what it means to come home to a kiss these days? It means you're in the wrong fucking house.

●

I've had one of those days – this morning I picked up my shirt and the button fell off; I picked up my briefcase and the handle fell off; I daren't go for a piss.

●

I've had a lazy day today. The wife asked me to go and see if it was raining out and I said, 'Fuck that – call the dog in and see if he's wet.'

●

My wife's legs have been giving her trouble lately. She came back from the doctor's the other day and I asked her how she'd got on. She said, 'Apparently my veins are too close together.' I said, 'I've never heard of that complaint.' 'Well, he told me I've got very-close veins.'

●

Mind you, I'm a bit worried about our doctor. I went to him because my foot kept going to sleep. He tied an alarm clock to my leg.

●

We were arguing at the breakfast table about our holidays, 'cause last year we went to Blackpool. The advertisement said the boarding house was three minutes from the sea, but I think it meant that Sebastian Coe stayed there the week before. What a place. We got up on the first morning and had a continental breakfast – we ate the quilt.

Our lass said, 'Did you hear that couple in the bedroom next door making a noise – sounded like she was having a fit.' I said, 'Yes, a tight bastard as well.'

●

I dread this bloody wet weather, don't you? It doesn't half grow the grass. Do you know I got up this morning and the grass and the nettles and the weeds were right up to my window sill. I was going to cut it, but why should I? I think that bastard in the flat below me should have a go first.

●

I've been having a terrible time with my back lately. I was playing piggyback with my three-year-old daughter and I fell off. So I went along to the doctor's to see if he could help me.

There was a woman sat next to me in the surgery and she looked a right sight. All the skin was off her knees and they were red raw. I said, 'What the bloody hell's happened to you, then?' She said, 'I was trying out doggie fashion.' I said, 'You'll have to do it the proper way now, won't you?' She thought for a minute and then replied, 'Well, I could, but I don't think the dog could.'

I finally got my turn to go into the doctor's. I took me trousers off and said, 'Have a look at this. My willie's like a walnut whip.' He said, 'You do realize that when you go for a piss you're supposed to shake it, not wring it out.' I said, 'That's all very well, doctor, but when I get into bed with my wife I just don't touch the sides at all.' He said, 'Do you drink lager, Chubby?' I nodded. 'Well, it shrivels things up, you know. You should drink Guinness for strength.' Some weeks later I rang the doctor to thank him. 'My sex life's A1!' He said, 'How much Guinness are you drinking, Chubby?' I said, 'I'm not. I've got the wife on lager.'

●

I leapt out of bed this morning – had to, it was on fire. I ran downstairs, and my wife was doing the breakfast in her slippers. I thought I must save up and get a pan. I said 'I'll have egg on toast.' She said, 'You'll have to, there's no plates left.' Then the phone went. This bloke on the line must have thought our house was a lighthouse, 'cause he asked me if the coast was clear.

Just then there was a knock on the door. I said, 'I hope that's your mother.' She said, 'Why?' I said, 'I've just cemented the step.' She cried, 'You hate my mother, don't you? Why do you wipe it off when she spits on you?' But when I tried to comfort her she cried even harder. 'Will you still love me when I get old?' she sobbed. 'Of course I do.'

In order to show willing I took her and her mother shopping. Well, her mother did nothing but moan. She was still moaning when she got out of the boot.

Hairy Pie

My isn't it warm, me balls are sticking to me legs.

•

If you wanna see me this summer, I'm doing two weeks in Scarborough with Anita Harris. If our lass finds out she'll go mad.

•

When I found out I was coming here to the Queens Social Club, I was about as excited as a blind poof in a hot-dog factory. I thought, the Queens Social, I'm sure to get fixed up. As I say, I'm Roy Brown and if you haven't seen me before I'm not bad looking for a comedian that's had his nose broken in three places: The Robin Hood and The Crown and Anchor.

•

I was fighting last night. Look at the teeth marks in me hand, look. But I'm not bothered, I've got his ear in me pocket.

•

She's as daft as arseholes our ma is. A funeral passed our house this morning. I happened to say: 'I wonder who's dead?' She said: 'I think it's the one in the box.'

And the wife's funny. She really is. We were arguing. I said: 'Come on, put that knife down, I'm boss in this house and don't you forget it.' I went on: 'Any more of your slabber and you'll make these beds yourself.' I mean, let's get something straight. I've done me making the beds for our lass. Then she helps me with the rest of the housework.

She was trying a new coat on this morning. I said, 'Your knickers are coming down.' She said: 'They're not.' I said: 'Well the coat's going back if they don't.'

•

Went into the butcher's and this woman picked a piece of meat up. She was looking at it and prodding it and poking it. The bloke behind the counter said: 'Oi, that's not your husband's dick. It won't get any bigger playing with it, ya know.'

•

I was walking behind two old ladies, and they were going for the bus, and they were rushing away. They must have passed the barber's shop. The door was open, and somebody was getting their hair singed. I heard one old lady say to the other one, 'Ooh, can you smell that, Martha?' Martha said: 'Yes, I think we're running too fast.'

•

Well, I suppose you're pretty excited, are ya, seeing as summer's on a fucking Wednesday this year. We went to Butlin's. We went along the A1, picked this hitchhiker up. Only fair, I'd knocked the fucker down. I stopped at a motorway cafe. Couldn't afford a full meal. I thought shall I have a sausage roll, two thousand fucking flies can't all be wrong.

The staff were having a bit of a party. Apparently one of the sandwiches was fourteen that day.

•

17

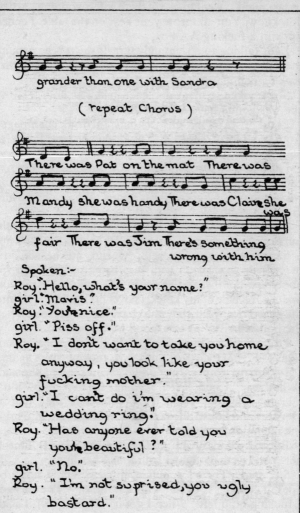

grander than one with Sandra

(repeat Chorus)

There was Pat on the mat There was Mandy she was handy There was Claire she was fair There was Jim There's something wrong with him

Spoken :-

Roy. "Hello, what's your name?"

girl. "Mavis."

Roy. "You're nice."

girl. "Piss off."

Roy. " I don't want to take you home anyway, you look like your fucking mother."

girl. "I can't do i'm wearing a wedding ring."

Roy. "Has anyone ever told you you're beautiful ?"

girl. "No."

Roy. " I'm not suprised, you ugly bastard."

We've had some good nights here. I wish you'd been with us last night. I went to one of these wife-swopping parties, you know. You all throw your keys on the table. I ended up with a fucking AA box.

I got talking to a right ugly tart. If she'd been around the same time as the Lord, there would have been another fucking commandment.

She smoked so many dog-ends in half an hour, I swore she was gonna have a shit in the street.

I said, 'If ya let me take ya home, I'll drink champagne from ya slipper.' She said: 'You'd soon be pissed, you fat cunt. I take a size twelve.'

I stopped the car on the outside of Middlesbrough. I came the old 'I've run out of petrol' routine. She said: 'Oh, what a shame, Chubby. I was gonna take you home and give ya a gobble.'

I said, 'You're not married, are ya?' She said, 'Oh yeah, our lad's in Durham Jail.' I said: 'Oh, okay then, he's not a hard case is he?' She said: 'Oh no, no, he was just depressed, you know, with him being unemployed for about six months, and he decided to rob the post office. So he put a pair of my knickers over his head and ran into the post office. Well, they must have turned him on. When the police arrived he was stood having a wank.'

I took her for a meal. She looked at the menu and said: 'I guess I'll have steak.' I said: 'Aye, fucking guess again.'

I called the waitress over. I said: 'Wine please.' She said: 'What year?' I said, 'Well, we'd like the fucker now if it's all right with you.' I said: 'I fancy this here, the Divinsor Devorey and Sons.' She said: 'That's the people who print the menu, dozy cunt.'

But to be honest with ya, I really liked this girl. I mean her pants were so tight I could read her lips.

She said: 'There's a bull over there. Oh, I hope he doesn't charge us.' I said: 'I hope he doesn't. I've only got a fucking quid left.' When I got her knickers off, I said: 'Now hang on a minute, you've got a bald fanny.' She said: 'Pardon?' I said: 'You've a bald minge, you've no

20

hairs.' She said: 'Do you wanna screw me or race fucking greyhounds?'

I felt sorry for her 'cause she'd just had a baby and it was a bit of a difficult birth. She had twenty stitches put in her mot. Shows you how big it was. There's only fucking eighteen in a potato sack.

What really annoyed me was she'd had the coil fitted and it was picking up the fucking CB. I was just gonna shove it up her arse, and this voice come from her fanny: 'That's a big Ten Four.'

●

A girl had a baby and she accused a young man of being the father. He denied this, but was summoned to appear in court. He told the magistrate that he couldn't be the father because, although he admitted he'd been with the girl, he was never properly in. The magistrate said, 'You must have been.' The young man said, 'Listen, if I popped my head round your front door, I wouldn't be in your house, would I?' The magistrate said, 'But you could spit a long way up the passage.'

●

An Irishman was making pretty good progress with a girl. She agreed to go away with him for a few days, provided he brought a sheath. When they went upstairs he admitted he didn't know how to wear it, so she rolled it down his thumb to show him. Then they put the light out and he got to work. After a while the girl said, 'You know I'm terribly sticky. I do believe you've broken that thing.' 'Oh no, I haven't,' he said as he put the light on. 'There it is, still on my thumb.'

●

A young woman was about to get married and she was still a virgin and pretty innocent. Her mother said, 'Before you go to bed on the first night, be sure and give him some oysters for supper.' Next day her mother asked her how

21

she had got on. 'Not very well. I suppose I lack your catering experience. I fed him a dozen oysters, but only nine worked.'

●

A policeman shone his torch into a graveyard at night and saw a courting couple making love. He brought them to court before the judge. 'And what were you doing in the graveyard at midnight?' asked the judge to the young man. 'Nothing, your Honour. Just burying a stiff.' 'What about you?' he said to the young girl. 'Your Honour, I was the undertaker.'

●

A man went to see his doctor about his memory. The doctor said, 'What makes you think you've lost your memory?' The man said, 'Well, I went home last night and when I was in bed the wife turned her back on me and said, 'You've had it,' and I couldn't remember if I had or not.

●

A young wife went to the doctor's. He said, 'Do you smoke after sex?' She replied, 'I don't know I've never looked.'

●

A young assistant in a chemist shop was rather sulky and abrupt with a customer, and the chemist said to him, 'Why don't you speak pleasantly to the customers when you're serving them?' The young man said, 'I never know what to say or talk about.' 'Well, talk about the weather.' The next customer to come in said, 'I want a packet of sanitary towels for the wife, please.' The young man remembered the boss's advice and as he handed over the parcel, he said, 'Looks like being a dull weekend, doesn't it?'

●

My wife was expecting a baby, and she went to the doctor's for a check-up. He stamped something small on her stomach with a rubber stamp. When she came home she showed it to me. 'What does it say?' I got my magnifying glass and had a look. It said: When you can read this with the naked eye, send for the midwife.

●

Two old maids went to the greengrocer's and enquired about the price of cucumbers. The shopkeeper said, 'Twenty-five pence each or three for sixty pence.' They looked at each other. 'Go on, Veronica. We can always eat one.'

●

A deb's sister wrote to her from America where she had gone to try her luck and improve the family's fortunes. She said that already she had bought a new fur coat, and it only cost her a hundred bucks. 'She never could spell,' said her sister.

●

A lady of the town was up before the bench. She was asked to declare her occupation and she said she was a dealer. 'What is that?' said the beak. 'Sir, it is old-established street trading.' 'I'm not having that,' said the beak. The learned clerk, who wanted to get on, said, 'Leave it to me, sir. I'll just put down that she's in the hole-sale business.'

●

On Monday morning a teacher asked three boys in his class, 'What was your mother doing when you left home this morning?' The first one said, 'Doing the washing, sir.' The second said, 'Doing the cleaning, sir.' The third said, 'Getting ready to go out and shoot pheasants.' 'What are you talking about?' said the teacher. 'Well, sir, me dad's left home and she threw her knickers in the fire and said she was going back on the game.'

●

23

Two men went behind a hedge to pee. Says one, 'I wish I had a big one like that. You're so big you can hold it with four fingers.' His pal paused, looked, and said, 'You're holding yours with four fingers. 'Yes, but three of them are getting wet.'

●

And of course you've heard about the 80-year-old man accused of rape but later acquitted because the evidence wouldn't stand up in court.

●

An American tourist found herself in conversation with a ruggedly handsome middle-aged Scot at a cocktail party. 'Excuse my bluntness,' she said, 'but is anything worn under the kilt?' 'Nay lassie,' he replied. 'It's as good as it ever was.'

●

Two cannibals were chatting over lunch. One said, 'You know, I just can't stand my mother-in-law.' 'Forget about her,' the other replied. 'Just eat the noodles.'

●

Don't drink and drive. You might hit a bump and spill it.

●

A rather inebriated fellow on the bus was tearing up a newspaper into tiny pieces and throwing them out of the window. 'Excuse me,' said the woman sitting next to him, 'but would you mind explaining why you are tearing up that paper and throwing the pieces out of the window?' It scares away the elephants,' said the drunk. 'I don't see any elephants,' said the woman smiling. 'Effective, isn't it?' said the drunk.

●

There's a wonderful new airline that is almost completely automated. You push a button and out comes your seat belt. You push a button on the seat belt and out comes your pillow. You push a button on your pillow and out comes the hostess. You push a button on the hostess and out come your teeth.

●

Fred's car glided to a halt on the edge of a lonely country road. 'I suppose,' said the pretty but reluctant date, 'you're going to pull the old petrol routine.' 'No,' said Fred, 'I'm going to pull the here-after routine.' 'The here-after routine? What's that?' she wanted to know. 'Well, if you're not here after what I'm after, then you're going to be here after I'm gone.'

●

The meanest Scotsman in the world was the one who fired a revolver on Christmas Eve and told his kids that Father Christmas had committed suicide.

●

A British anthropologist was doing some research in an isolated African village, and the local tribal leader asked if he would like to attend a trial of his people that they were conducting that afternoon. 'I think you'll be surprised,' said the chief, 'at how we have copied your country's legal procedures. You see we have read the accounts of many English trials in your newspapers.'

When the scientist arrived at the crudely constructed courthouse, he was indeed amazed at how closely the African court officials resembled those of his native land. Both counsels were suitably attired in long black robes and the traditional white powdered wigs worn by all British counsels, but he could not help being puzzled by the occasional appearance of a bare-breasted tribal maiden who ran through the crowded courtroom, waving her arms frantically.

After the trial the anthropologist congratulated his host on what he had seen and then asked, 'What was the purpose of having a semi-nude woman run through the courtroom during the trial?' 'No purpose,' replied the chief, 'but all the accounts we read in the papers about the British trials invariably mention something about an excited titter, running through the gallery. . . .'

●

A man rushed into a pub in a rather agitated state. 'Does anyone own a large black cat with a white collar?' he asked, somewhat nervously. There was no reply. 'Does anyone own a big black cat with a white collar?' asked the man again, raising his voice even higher above the general noise of the bar. But still no one answered the question. 'Oh dear,' muttered the man, 'I must have run over the vicar.'

●

There were two babies in a pram. One turned to the other and said, 'Are you a little girl or a little boy?' 'I don't know,' was the giggled reply. 'I can tell,' said the first baby gleefully, and dived beneath the covers and then resurfaced. 'You're a girl and I'm a boy,' he announced proudly. 'That's clever,' said the baby girl. 'How could you tell?' 'Easy, you've got pink booties and I've got blue ones.'

●

The cannibal came home to find his wife chopping up snakes and a very small man. 'Oh, no,' he groaned. 'Not snake and pygmy pie again.'

●

A young man was visiting London when he saw an advertisement for a restaurant which claimed that any dish requested could be served. The man decided to visit the restaurant in order to test the validity of their claim. When he was seated at the table he asked the waiter for elephant ears on toast. The waiter took his order calmly and went away to the kitchen. A few minutes later the waiter returned and said, 'I do apologize, but we've run out of bread.'

●

When I lived in lodgings my landlady kept some animals in the yard at the back of the house. The first day I was there one of the chickens died, so we had chicken soup. The next day the pig died, so we had pork chops. The following day the duck died, so we had roast duck and apple sauce. The next day the landlady's husband died . . . so I left.

●

Two little boys were paddling in the sea. 'Coo, ain't your feet dirty,' said one little boy. 'Yes,' came the reply. 'We didn't come to the seaside last year.'

●

First patient: 'I see they've brought in another case of diarrhoea.'
Second patient: 'That's good, anything's better than that awful lemonade they've been giving us.'

●

A young man walked into the pet shop and asked if he could buy 387 beetles, 18 rats and 5 mice. 'I'm sorry, sir, but we can only supply the mice. What do you require all the creatures for?' asked the pet-shop manager. 'I was thrown out of my flat this morning,' came the reply, 'and my landlady says I must leave the place exactly as I found it.'

●

For years Amy Clegg's parrot had not said a single word, and eventually she became convinced it was a stupid parrot unable to learn to speak English. Then one day as she was feeding it a piece of lettuce as a special treat, the parrot suddenly squawked, 'There's a maggot on it, there's a maggot on it.' Amy Clegg was astonished. 'You can talk,' she exclaimed. 'But why haven't you spoken before?' 'Oh,' replied the parrot, 'the food's been excellent up to now.'

•

I learned to swim at a very early age. When I was three my parents used to row me out to sea in a little boat until they got about a mile or so away from the shore, and then throw me out. I had to swim back. I quite liked the swim, but it was getting out of the sack that was difficult.

•

Hello, is that the police station? Yes. Have any lunatics escaped near here recently? Not that I know of, sir, why do you ask? Someone's run off with my wife.

•

I'm worried, Doctor. I keep thinking I'm a pair of curtains.
Stop worrying and pull yourself together.

•

A small boy was absent from school for two days. When he finally showed up his teacher asked him why he had been away from school. 'Sorry, miss,' he said. 'My dad got burnt.' 'Oh,' said the teacher, 'nothing serious, I hope.' 'No, miss. They don't mess about at the crematorium.'

•

One Sunday the vicar was explaining the difference between knowledge and faith to his congregation. 'In the front row,' he said, 'we have Mr Jones and his wife, and three children. Now she knows they are her children: that's knowledge. He believes they are his children: that's faith.'

•

28

A Scotsman was fined for indecent conduct at Edinburgh. According to witnesses the man continually wiped the perspiration off his forehead with his kilt.

•

Man (to newsboy): Give me a *Sun*. *Newsboy*: Whaddya think I am, the stork?

•

Two things you can be sure of in life: death and taxes. There's one thing about death. It doesn't go up every time there's a Budget.

•

First man: My brother is a very clever scientist. He crossed a peach with a plum and got a nectarine.
Second man: That's not all that brilliant. My uncle crossed a locomotive with an automobile and got a funeral.

•

My girl was standing in my uncle's corn field. She was so skinny, she looked like a scarecrow. She frightened the crows so much they brought back the corn they had stolen three days before.

•

First woman: I've got a new boyfriend now. You'll have to meet him.
Second woman: What's he like?
First woman: Oh, whisky, gin, anything.

•

She had a head like a doorknob. Any man can turn it.

•

Man: How much do you charge to take children's photographs?
Photographer: Five pounds a dozen.
Man: You'll have to give me more time. I only have ten now.

●

A father was shopping in a department store with his small daughter when the little girl suddenly pulled on his coat sleeve and said: 'Daddy, I gotta go.' 'In a few minutes, dear,' the father replied. 'I gotta go now!' the little girl insisted in a loud voice. To avoid a scene a saleslady stepped forward and said, 'That's all right, sir. I'll take her for you.' So they hurried off hand in hand to the ladies' room. When they returned the father asked the daughter, 'Did you thank the nice lady for being so kind?' 'Why should I thank her?' retorted the little girl as loud as before. 'She had to go too.'

●

'I know how babies are made,' boasted one small fry to another. 'That's nothing,' the second small fry replied. 'I know how they're not.'

●

The little boy pointed to two dogs in the park and asked his father, 'What are they doing?' 'They are making puppies, son.' That night the boy wandered into his parents' room while they were making love. The little boy asked, 'What are you doing, dad?' The father replied, 'Making you a baby brother.' 'Gee, dad,' the boy said. 'Turn her over. I'd rather have a puppy.'

●

I might tell you I got out of a sick bed to be here tonight. My girlfriend's got flu.

●

I come from an old military family. My great-great-grandfather fell at Waterloo. Somebody pushed him off Platform Five.

●

The day I was born my father went round and gave everyone a cigar. Mine was a little strong, but I got through it.

●

When I was a kid my father used to take me out in a red velveteen jacket and matching knickerbockers. He did look a scream.

●

Musical History of Marriage:
The courtship: 'Temptation'; wedding night: 'Tonight's the Night'; the honeymoon: 'Night and Day'; ten years later: 'Some of These Days'; twenty years later: 'Just One More Chance'; forty years later: 'Memories'.

●

First man: I was married twice, and I'll never marry again. First wife died after eating poison mushrooms, and my second died of a fractured skull.
Second man: That's a shame, How did that happen?
First man: She wouldn't eat her mushrooms.

●

There was a band leader who spent all week working on a new arrangement and then discovered that his wife wasn't going away on holiday on her own after all.

●

'I think you've made a mistake with my bill,' said the patron in the bar. 'You've only charged me 50p for three large whiskies.' 'No mistake,' said the bartender. 'Fantastic,' said the patron. 'But how can you afford to operate such a plush bar? Are you the owner?' 'No,' confided the barman. 'The owner's upstairs with my wife. And what he's doing to her up there, I'm doing to his business down here.'

●

Have you heard about the man who never worried about his marriage until he moved from Norwich to Manchester, and found he still had the same milkman.

●

Did you hear about the little boy who had a Pakistani father and a Scottish mother? They called him Pakamac.

●

Paddy found a milk churn in the hedge, and thought it was a cow's nest.

●

Paddy's prize on the 'Generation Game': a conveyor belt and two sliding doors.

●

Paddy bought a paper shop. It blew away.

●

Paddy wanted to buy a house, so he went to British Home Stores.

●

What do you call a paddy on a bike? Dope peddler.

●

A 20-year-old girl married an 80-year-old millionaire: hard times were certainly over for her.

●

It was so hot last summer, we fed the chickens cracked ice to keep them from laying hard-boiled eggs.

●

Englishman: If you're so cold, why don't you try using a hot-water bottle?
Irishman: I tried that and it didn't work, I couldn't get my feet in the neck of the bottle.

●

'What would you like for Christmas,' the sophisticated parents asked their young son. 'I wanna watch.' So they let him.

●

During a visit to the zoo the inquisitive child asked, 'Mummy, how do lions make love?' 'I don't know, dear,' replied the mother. 'Most of your father's friends are Rotarians.'

●

The sophisticated lady was approached on the dance floor by a gentleman slightly her junior. 'I'm sorry,' she said in a superior tone, 'but I couldn't dance with a child.' 'Oh, I'm sorry,' he said. 'I didn't know your condition.'

●

'How did you like your stay in the nudist camp?' asked one bachelor to another. 'Well,' came the reply, 'the first three days were the hardest.'

●

'Why do you lower your eyes when I say I love you?' the young man asked the attractive girl in the nudist camp. 'To see if it's true,' she replied.

●

Then there was the little old lady with varicose veins who won first prize at the costume ball. She went in the nude as a road map.

●

I know a feller whose feet were so big that even when he danced with Raquel Welch he stepped on her toes.

●

The theatrical agent was trying to sell a new strip act to a nightclub manager. He raved about the girl's unbelievable 72.26.40 figure. 'What kind of dance does she do?' asked the manager, duly impressed. 'Well, she doesn't actually dance at all,' the agent replied. 'She just crawls about the stage and tries to stand up.'

●

A pink elephant strolled into a bar. 'You're a little early today,' said the barman. 'He ain't here yet.'

●

When I asked a zoologist friend of mine how porcupines have sex I was told, 'Very carefully, very carefully.'

●

Two small mice were crouched under a table in a chorus girls' dressing room. 'Wow,' exclaimed the first mouse. 'Have you ever seen so many gorgeous legs in your life?' 'Means nothing to me,' said the second. 'I'm a titmouse.'

●

'Excuse me, sorr,' said the Irishwoman. 'Are you a plastic surgeon?' 'Well, yes, I am.' 'Then could you put a new handle on my pedal-bin?'

●

I'm not saying that our house is damp, but where else would you find free-range goldfish.

●

I would not say that my wife is bitchy, but she is the only woman I know who's been sick with distemper.

●

Then there was the Irishman who rang reception for room service, and they sent up two vicars and a dozen choir boys.

●

A fellow was bragging how his wife could sing. 'Last night she got up to C and held it for three minutes.' 'That's nothing,' said his friend. 'My wife got up to P. Couldn't find the pot, and held it all night.'

●

The waiter served four men every day for lunch, and every day they would play a joke on him. One day they would put his tip in the gravy, and so on. After a while they gave him a big tip and said they would play no more jokes on him. 'Fair enough,' he replied. 'And from now on I'll not spit in your coffee.'

●

What do you get if you cross an Irishman with a pig? Thick bacon.

●

What do you do if an Irishman throws a handgrenade at you? Pull out the pin and throw it back.

●

How can you tell a level-headed Irishman? He dribbles from both sides of his mouth.

●

Heard about the Irish tap-dancer? He fell in the sink.

●

I recently attended a wedding where the bride was six months' pregnant. The guests all threw puffed rice.

•

Before retiring on his wedding night, the young minister turned to his bride and murmured, 'Pardon me, darling, I'm going to pray for guidance.' 'Sweetheart,' his wife answered, 'I'll take care of the guidance, you pray for endurance.'

•

The research department informs us that today's most common form of marriage proposal is: You're what?

•

For twenty long and wonderful years my wife and I were deliriously happy. Then we met.

•

Tony arrived at his office late one morning and was greeted with giggles from the pretty receptionist. 'Why are you laughing at me?' he asked. 'There's a big black smudge on your face,' said the girl. 'Oh, that's easy to explain. I saw my wife off on a month's holiday this morning and I kissed her goodbye.' 'But what about the smudge?' 'As soon as she got on the train I ran up and kissed the engine too.'

•

Saturday was to be the day of Joe's wedding, and he and his father were enjoying a nightcap together before they retired to gather strength for the next day's event. Lifting his glass in a toast to his father, Joe asked, 'Any advice before I take the big step, Dad?' 'Yes,' said his father. 'Two things. First, insist on having a night out with the boys.' 'Makes sense. And the second?' 'The second. Don't waste it on the boys.'

•

An undertaker called the next of kin to confirm the funeral arrangements desired for the dear departed, and as luck would have it the son-in-law, who was actually delighted to be rid of the old battle-axe, answered the phone. 'We are sorry to disturb you in this time of personal grief,' the undertaker intoned solemnly, 'but there appears to be some confusion as to whether the body of the loved one is to be buried or cremated. 'Let's take no chances,' said the son-in-law. 'Let's do both.'

●

I know a young thing who has been married three times and is still a virgin. Her first husband, a psychiatrist, only talked about it. The second was a gynaecologist who just looked at it. The third was a gourmet and he. . . .

●

I once took the wife to Newcastle and she wanted to stay at the Hotel Yumca. I said, 'That's the YMCA, you daft cunt.' We booked into one hotel and the manager said, 'A fiver each and a fiver for the dog.' When I pointed out we hadn't got a dog, he said, 'I know, we have and you've got his fucking room.' I said, 'Do you mind if I look round?' He said, 'You look round to me, fat fucker.'

I once put two aspirins on the wife's tongue when she was asleep. She woke up with a start, 'What you doing? I haven't got a headache.' I said, 'Good. Any chance of a fuck then?'

She once said I want the bathroom ceiling decorating and I said whoever invented decorating wants fucking, she said, you didn't say that last night when you were up my arse did you, it was whoever invented fucking wanted decorating.

She asked me to go next door and borrow a paintbrush from Maureen. Well, Maureen's always in, so I looked through the window. What a shock! The milkman's up her arse, the coalman's sucking her tits, and the paper lad's getting a gobble. I rushed back to tell the wife. She said, 'She's the same at the bingo, a right lucky bastard.'

The wife bought her mother a toaster. I chipped in and bought her a slice of bread.

My wife's not a great one for cooking. One evening after work I said to her, 'What's for dinner?' She said, 'Salad with rhubarb to follow.' Showing willing I said, 'Oh good, where is it?' She handed me a trowel and said, 'At the bottom of the garden.' I lost my temper then. 'When a man comes home at night he's entitled to a hot meal.' She said, 'You're in luck, the bin's on fire.'

I said, 'Get your knickers off now and get in that back bedroom, I'm just in the mood to ride the fucking arse off yer.' She said, 'No, we'll have it in the kitchen, I'd like to boil an egg.' I put my hand straight down her draws. She smiled. 'Do you want your palm read?' I said, 'Why, are you a clairvoyant?' She said, 'No, I've just come on.' She backed away and said, 'By the way I've gone into a tree with the car.' I said, 'How did you manage that?' She said, 'It wasn't my fault, I beeped the horn. Anyway, I had to take my knickers off for the policeman.' I said, 'You must be fucking joking.' 'No,' she said, 'something about measuring the skid marks.'

●

We had an accident in the car and we received some money off the insurance. Mind you, only because I had common sense to kick our lass's teeth in before the police got there.

●

I got home, had a cup of Horlicks, accidently pissed on the cat and it fell asleep. My wife shouted down the stairs, 'Is that you, my little flower-pot?' I said, 'It fucking better be me!' I got into bed and said, 'My it's fucking coming in cold.' She said, 'It's bloody well not – you can warm it up with your hands first.' She said, 'Your daughter brought

38

her boyfriend home tonight. I said, 'So what?' 'Oh! he only smoked your fags, drank your lager and they were putting their tongues in each other's mouths and the settee was rocking from side to side and I couldn't watch "Dynasty".' I said, 'We all did that when we were young.' 'Oh, yeah, but you didn't wipe your cock on the velvet curtains.'

●

I live on a rough estate. My house is only a stone's throw from the sea – you can easily tell because all the fucking windows are broken. There's that many break-ins on our estate you're liable to trap somebody's fingers when you are closing the windows. There must be twenty muggings a week. I once went to the fish shop round the corner and a fella jumped out with a knife. He must have been a local lad, the knife still had butter on.

There's a fella lives next door who must be 6ft 12in. I'm frightened to death of him. Their twelve kids patted our dog to death. You could never raid their bonfire as they kept it in the living room. The same fella once went into a jewellers' shop and tossed his cock on the counter. The girl behind the counter never flinched. She calmly said, 'Excuse me, this is a clock shop not a cock shop.' He grinned and said, 'I know, get a couple of hands on that.'

●

I called in the hairdresser's the other day and he said, 'You know, Chubby, if I shaved all your hair off no one would recognize you.' I said, 'You shave all my hair off and no one will recognize you.' Isn't it funny, though, when you're in the hairdresser's and you're talking – they love to talk – and he says, 'Where are you going for your holidays?' And you say, 'Oh, I'm going to Disneyland for seventeen days. It'll cost us about £1000.' He boasts, 'We're going to the Bahamas for three weeks.' Next week you bump into him at Whitley Bay.

●

Verse 1

There's a crazy new dance that's sweepin' the place it's a public disgrace to the human race pull your knickers down & cock your arse in the air if the feeling's right you can do it anywhere ———— Back

CHORUS

Scuttle it's called the Back Scuttle Oh ——— Oh Back Scuttle

2

This new rhythm was heaven sent You can do it even if your bent Legs apart take off your clothes Close your eyes and touch your toes Back

(Repeat Chorus)

Spoken:-

Get on down Yowza Yowza Yowza
Click with a chick or you'll get no dick
Feel the balls in and out
I aint fussy shake your pussy

Verse 4

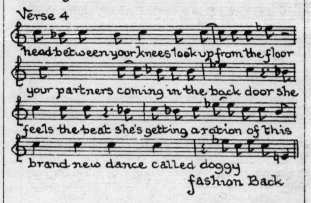

head between your knees look up from the floor

your partners coming in the back door she

feels the beat she's getting a ration of this

brand new dance called doggy
fashion Back

(Repeat Chorus)

Spoken :-
Have you noticed all women look the
same from the back
C'mon get your drawers off
I'll do you a bit of good
Dont call me fat arse
I'll put my foot up your bottom
Give you a boot scuttle

Everyone knows me as Roy Brown, but that's not my name, it's Aday Brown. When I was born my dad looked in the cot and said, 'Let's call it a day.' I have two half brothers and a half sister, then my mother took the saw away from me. My parents didn't want me. Every time I had a bath they'd put things in it like the electric fire. They once bought me a rattle for Christmas – there was a snake on the other fucking end of it.

You couldn't play 'I Spy' in our house, there was fuck all to spy. Dad came home in the fog one night and said, 'It's pea soup out there.' We all shouted, 'Great! We're getting something to eat!'

●

I once went to a club so far off the beaten track Lord Lucan was playing the organ. I think the drummer's last job was with Idi Amin's firing squad. What a filthy club – there was so much broken glass in the lounge even the Alsatians wore slippers. I said to the owner, 'This wallpaper looks flocked.' 'Don't be silly, it's good for another couple of years yet,' he said. I went into the gents and the soap was on a chain.

I got talking to a right posh lady, a Mrs Kipling. She was an exceedingly good fuck. She loved to fantasize. One night she opened her legs and said, 'Come here and pretend it's a garage.' I nearly lost me back wheels. She said, 'I bet you'd like to see where I had my operation.' I said, 'Bloody hell, would I.' She said, 'That's the hospital over there.'

I said to her, 'You aren't married, are you, 'cos you're not wearing a wedding ring.' She said, 'I'll be honest with you, Chubby, the fella I marry will smoke Havana cigars, have money in the bank, drive a big flash car and have a twelve-inch cock.' Well, that rules me out, I don't smoke cigars.

●

Can you imagine what fish smelt like before women went swimming in the sea?

●

I hope there's such a thing as reincarnation and I come back as one of Charlie's Angels Tampax's. Knowing my luck I'll come back as Bosley's jock strap.

●

You are what you are in life. If you take after your family, if your mother and father bring you up right, you don't become a bastard like me. The best part of being a bastard is you don't have to buy a present on Father's Day. I was a test-tube baby: my father was a wanker. Every year I send a card to the chemical division at ICI. I felt sorry for my dad. There wasn't much call for his trade, chariot-making. My mother reckons when the *Mary Rose* came up his bait-box was on it.

●

I took a tart to the ABC the other night, to see a film about a 12-year-old girl. It was called 'First Blood'.

There's a couple in front of us snogging on and they're putting their tongues in each other's mouths, and he got so excited this bloke, his toupée came off and fell on the floor. He's groping about and accidentally puts his hand up her skirt. She goes 'Oohh, that's it.' He says 'No, mine hasn't got a parting in the middle.'

I took her home, we walked through the cemetery. I said, 'You're not frightened are ya?' She said, 'No.' I said, 'Would you mind going first then?'

I kissed her on the doorstep. She said, 'Why don't you kiss me on the mouth like everybody else does?' I said, 'Fuck off.'

I said, 'If you're so cocksure of your fucking self get in the car.' I took her up Skippers Land at Normanby. We were lying completely naked in the back of the car with fuck all on, and I looked up and I saw this bobby's helmet. This copper said, 'What's going on here?' I said

'Nought.' He said, 'Here, hold me fucking torch.'

I took her back to her house. I said, 'Can I come in?' She said, 'Oh, Mum's a light sleeper. She sleeps with the light on.' 'Oh,' I said, 'I'm a hard sleeper. I sleep with the fucking window open.'

I had to pack her in for health reasons. Our lass were gonna fucking kill us.

I bought her one of these greaseproof brassieres for Christmas. Doesn't make your tits any bigger, but it keeps what you've got fresh.

●

I went to a party over Christmas and I'm not kidding you, I've been to some fucking parties but I've never seen so much fanny in my life. Ended up with some fucking tupperware.

They were playing this music, and when it stopped you had to grab a tart and kiss her. Everybody's pissed, so when the music stopped I grabbed this tart and I stuck my lips on her. I said, 'Come 'ere you.' She followed me about all night. I know what you're thinking, Chubby, you lying bastard, you're not that good as a kisser. She was doing the cartwheel at the time. I wondered why she had black stockings on her arms, and a fucking hairy face. Any road her breath stunk. She'd knock a fly off a bucket of shite.

●

Well, I don't know what it is about women, but they're such dirty bastards aren't they. I mean, I'm lying in bed with her last night and she wants a piss. So she goes for a slash and deliberately leaves the fucking door open. I'm listening to her, and she's sssssshhhhhhh. When she comes back she knees me in the side, elbows me in the face, cocks her legs over, little drops of piss all over me. I said, 'You must be Teeside's dirtiest cunt.' She said, 'I haven't got a cock so I can't shake it.' I said, 'Well stamp your fucking feet then.'

I think she's seeing another bloke. I come home the

other day and said to her, 'There's a nude jogger in our garden. I wonder what he's doing that for?' She said, 'Because you fucking come home early.'

I caught her in bed with a bloke. I said, 'Who the fucking hell's that?' She said, 'I don't know, he's a new one on me.'

She once fucked off with the butcher. She said he had bigger joints. Come crawling back like they always do. 'Will ya take us back. I've been with other men.' I said, 'So have I. Fucking turn over.'

She's trying to impress me now. She's taken up knitting and made me a lovely V-neck pair of socks.

She rips all ma best clothes up so I can't go out. I bet we're the only house in our street with a polo-neck floor cloth.

She started making all her own clothes. She said, 'What do ya think of this dress?' I said, 'It'll look better when the potatoes are in it.'

●

I was in the garden this morning, keeping a look-out while the wife siphoned the petrol out of next door's lawnmower, and that neighbour of mine came over. 'Hey, Chubby, your fucking dog keeps going for me.' I said, 'Do ya wanna buy him, he won't go any fucking where for us.'

●

Mind you, I always watch ma 'p's and 'q's when I come round 'ere 'cause there's some fucking hard lads in Scarborough, isn't there? I walked out the club last time and said to this bloke, 'Excuse me, where can I get some cheap digs round 'ere? He went, 'Ooh ya fucking bastard.'

●

I got a flat tyre, and while I'm changing the wheel this cheeky cunt jumped in the car and starts unscrewing the dashboard. I said, 'What the fucking hell's going on?' He said, 'If you're having the tyres, I'm having the cassette and radio.'

●

This woman went to the funeral parlour. She said, 'My name's Robinson.' This chap said, 'Eehh, I'm terribly sorry Mrs Robinson, but when we were preparing your husband we couldn't get the coffin lid down 'cause his cock was so big, so we've amputated it.' She said, 'I hope you haven't thrown it away.' He said, 'No, we've placed it between the cheeks of his arse just so he'll rest in peace.' 'Oh,' she said. 'Can I have a look at him?' So they walked over to the coffin and he lifted the lid up. When she looked in the coffin, she swore there was a tear in his eye. She said, 'It fucking hurts; ya bastard, doesn't it!'

●

I came on the bus tonight. I said to the conductor, 'Do ya stop at the Grand?' She said, 'What? On my fucking wages.'

When I got on the bus at Middlesbrough, twenty West Indians got off. They must have thought I was a fucking ghost.

●

The wife's started this keep-fit routine. She said to me this morning, 'I've just done the splits twenty-five times.' I said, 'Well, personally, I think that's fucking stretching it a bit.'

I took her for a meal, I'll never forget it. The waiter came over and he must have known who I was. 'Hi, Chubby, what would you like.' I said, 'Surprise me.' He showed us a photo of our lass in the fucking nude.

I said, 'Could ya keep the bill under a fiver.' He gave us a knife and fork each and said the slop bucket's out the back.

She didn't half show me up. I said, 'Put your knickers on, the fucking pound's for the waiter.'

Pissefenie

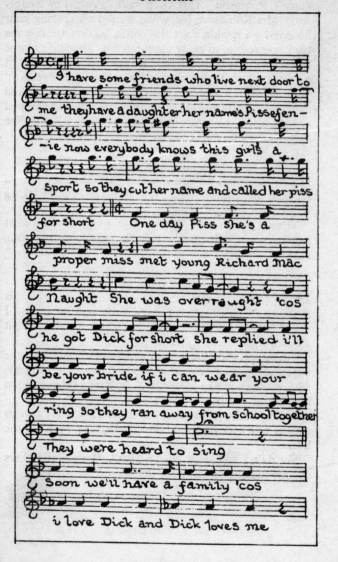

I have some friends who live next door to
me they have a daughter her name's Pissefen-
-ie now everybody knows this girls a
sport so they cut her name and called her piss
for short   One day Piss she's a
proper miss met young Richard Mac
Naught She was overraught 'cos
he got Dick for short she replied i'll
be your bride if i can wear your
ring so they ran away from school together
They were heard to sing
Soon we'll have a family 'cos
i love Dick and Dick loves me

47

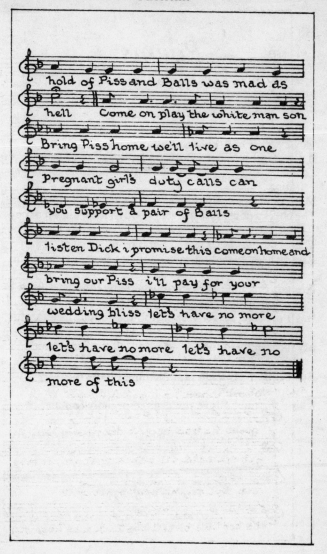

Poems

My Body

If I were to make my body and start all over again
I'd make a much smaller belly and a much much larger
  brain.
My legs aren't really hairy – they'd do for a start.
The cheeks of my arse are very good friends, but even they
  must part.
This nose I've got is not so hot it reminds me of a cherry,
And on a foggy night it gets so bright and people think I'm
  merry.
I've got this hole in my skin where the food goes in. It's
  convenient to walk
But I'd make bigger feet so my toes could meet and it
  would be easier to talk.
My face isn't bad for a 40-year-old lad. I mean, I wouldn't
  like to be thin,
But being overweight is something I hate, this way I use
  more skin.
I visit the pub; I love my grub, especially fish and chips
  when they're hot.
I don't think I'll change my body – I'll do with the bastard
  I've got.

Dick Teasing

Don't mention that word suspender, I go all weak at the
  knees.

It's not my fault I was thirty-five before I was told about
the birds and the bees.
Don't mention that word brassiere, my underpants are
starting to itch,
Play the white man, don't say tights, now you're being a
bitch.
Don't mention that word pantie girdle, see-through
nightie as well,
Don't bend over in front of me, at my age it gives me hell.
Don't mention the pubic, I feel stiff right down below,
Please don't talk with your mouth full. Oh God, it's
gonna blow.

A Date

When me and my pal went courting, you know it was
supposed to be tit for tat,
But the girls I got didn't offer a lot. They'd be thin, they'd
be short or fat.
I remember this date with two tarts and they both lived in
our street,
And one had a big reputation, about the same size as her
feet.
We went to the pub on the corner for a drink and a bite to
eat, nothing more,
Mine choked on the pie, out came her glass eye and
started to roll on the floor.
To show that I wasn't a coward I picked up this eye, it was
big
And a piece of loose thread caught the side of her head,
accidentally pulled off her wig.
She thanked me and bent down to kiss me. It was only a
friendly peck.
I thought what a cheek that I couldn't speak 'cos her
dentures were stuck in my neck.
She stood up to go to the ladies, bashed right in my face
with her knee.

'Are you feeling a draught?' I cried, then I laughed, ''Cos
    your knickers are down here with me.'
I said to my pal, 'Look, I'm leaving, this girl's just coming
    to bits,
She's false eyelashes and a wig, she's a bit of a pig, and the
    flat-chested bastard's no tits.'
My pal said, 'Stop moaning, for fuck's sake. How often
    do you usually score?'
I said, 'With any luck this thing that I've took I could get
    home and give it what for.'

The Transvestite

I know, but it's not what your thinking, it looks bad, I
    won't deny that –
You caught me red-handed. I'm clumsy, don't say it, I
    know I am a twat.
The truth is I really didn't mean it and now I feel out of
    place.
It wasn't quite right, it was wrong on the night. Your back
    was turned so now I'm two-faced.
I feel awful. Does that answer your question? So I'm
    guilty, I've committed a sin.
Stop staring that way or I'll walk away, you went out, you
    should have stopped in.
It won't happen again, this I promise, I'll be careful, I
    won't be so blunt.
Not only is it one of your brassieres, but I'm wearing the
    cunt back to front.

What a Night

I came home at teatime, she said she'd be alone.
She said he was a nudist who'd come to use the phone.
She said he had a button loose and was only trying to
    please,
You know, biting off the loose cotton with being down on
    her knees.

I said 'You've no knickers on.' She said, 'Oh! I've forgotten them, I thought the room was too warm.'

Then I found this French letter floating in my stew.

They're fucking bastards, these butchers, I mean, they're very hard to chew.

I finished my tea, then off to the club. I'm a comic; it's my bread and butter.

I was on with this act that ate razor blades, you think I'm a nutter.

The beer tasted like cat's piss, the piano player was a queer called Rose,

The drummer had only one arm, you know, and a fucking big boil on his nose.

The stripper's tattoo was so funny, on her bum was only this wheel

But when she bent over it revealed a Land-Rover and all the lads wanted a feel.

I walked on the stage in the darkness, and doing my act with no lights

They started to boo at a joke that was blue, you know I died on my arse that night.

So I'm stood in front of the committee and they'd all just got out of jail.

'The zip was broke on your trousers, son, we could see the size of your tail.

'You're not very good for a comedian. You pissed in the sink, that's a farce.

'We've restricted your pat. Have you anything to say?'
'Aye, stick your club up your arse.'

The Stag Night

It's a wonderful thing, a stag night. When the stripper removes her clothes.

You see more than you bargained for when she touches her toes.

You've told the wife it's business, you won't be home till late.

Probably sitting there with a hard-on, frightened to tell
  your mate.
It's a wonderful thing, a stag night, glancing at private
  parts.
They usually put on pies and peas so the room's full of
  noisy farts.
You can't help getting excited, it's the girls you've got to
  thank.
I walked into the toilet, the bastard was having a wank.
It's a wonderful thing, a stag night, you are back to the bar
  again.
The drink's coming out of your ears, and it's only half
  past ten.
The comic just told a story about a fanny that's never been
  kissed.
You don't think it's very funny but you'll be laughing
  because you're pissed.
It's a wonderful thing, a stag night, when the comic's got
  you in fits,
You can't beat a nice hairy arse and a massive pair of tits.

The Piano

Sharps and flats running up the scale:
Practise a tune till you hit it on the nail.
Keys and more keys, morning, noon and night:
Don't give up practising till you've got it right.
First time in public, this is what it takes.
Your friends are only listening to see if you make mistakes.
Pretend you're at the Albert Hall,
It's you they've come to see.
Take a little simple song
And play the twat in C.
C is a lovely white scale –
It's prestigious, you see,
But D has nasty black notes
That live next door to E.
E has four more black notes,

D note's next of kin,
Which upsets their friendly F,
Because the walls are thin.
G comes next, a lovely sound,
With one sharp proud and fine,
No relation to big A with three sharps marking time.
Last of all, guess who with five black sharps, it's B.
Thank God I've got that over,
Now I can get back to C.

The Supporter

I'm not very keen on my local team, and I know it's sad to
    slander Gruesome Park,
But the club's not very rich, so the bottles on the pitch get
    cashed in for players after dark.
The great days have passed now, the corner flag's half-
    massed,
And on Saturdays
I always take the wife because the teams we play don't
    mark you straight away,
But they do end up marking you for life.
Shirts out, socks in, start to pass the ball around,
The trainers trembling on the bench,
For their forward's all set to make a hole in our net, so our
    goalie's dug himself a trench.
We were winning at half-time and the crowd suspected
    crime,
So a dope test was called for pretty fast.
I'd knew I'd have to fly for an Oxo and a pie.
The result was in the end our players passed.
When our lads are winning, all the crowd are grinning.
It looks as if the team are on the mend.
We are giving them a fright, because we are playing like
    dynamite,
But even dynamite goes up in the end.
Well, we lost again, someone blamed the rain.
Should have been called off in this monsoon.

The true supporters bring their wellies;
They don't sit home and watch the tellies.
Yes, I'm here every Saturday afternoon.

'News of the World'

It's called the *News of the World*, perverted readers all
    enjoy
'Three nuns in a bed with a monk', and 'man interferes
    with a boy',
'Girl raped in the back of a car', 'transvestite caught',
    that's life.
And the coalman's having a hell of a time, he's fucked off
    with the milkman's wife.
'Homosexual Bill just been passed', next page reads 'men
    for kicks',
Beats me why they bother with arseholes, when AIDs is
    rotting their dicks.
Yes, this *News of the World* is the paper, it's the reporters
    you have to thank.
I mean, look at this on the sports page:
The England manager enjoying a wank.

Marriage

My wife makes life a living hell,
We never get on very well.
She rations sex once a week
Because she is strong and I am meek.
I kissed her cheek, I said she's mine,
She was bending over at the time,
Her foot comes up, then diverts, and lands in a place that
    hurts.
I'm charging you from this day on.
But you're my wife, we have a son,
Besides I'm broke, does that make sense?
C'mon, I'll lend you fifty pence,

56

Don't make a noise, silly clown,
More excuses get me down.
Things are different when your canned,
You relieve your tensions with your hand.

Silly Cow

In meadows where the grass is green,
I have a tale to tell
About a cow called Daisy.
You often hear her bell;
She was a credit to the farm.
But a virgin's life is dull,
Until one day a cockerel introduced her to a bull.
They stared at one another –
She never knew her fate.
It happened on the morning 'cause someone had left open
    the gate,
In he came like a bull in a china shop.
The trouble was the stupid bull didn't know where to
    stop,
Poor Daisy, she didn't know, she got too much too soon.
You must know the feeling, girls, coming back off your
    honeymoon.
All in one she took it, she nearly came to bits.
It's Daisy's fault for having a lovely pair of tits.
I watched his face full of joy, he leads a life so full.
When I come back, I want to be a bull.

●

There once was a jolly old bloke
Who picked up a girl for a poke.
He took down her pants,
Fucked her into a trance,
and then shit in her shoe for a joke.

●

57

A young lady who taught at Devizes.
Was had up at the local assizes
For teaching young boys
Matrimonial joys
And giving French letters as prizes.

●

There was a young fellow from Leeds
Who swallowed a package of seeds.
Great tufts of grass
Sprouted out of his arse,
And his balls were all covered with weeds.

●

There was a young man of Australia
Who painted his arse like a dahlia.
The drawing was fine, the colour divine.
The scent – ah, that was a failure.

One Liners

We called the dog Drambuie 'cause he was a good liquor!

●

Our neighbour said: 'Your dog's shit in our garden!' I said: 'It's all right, I've got a licence.' He said, 'I've got a marriage licence, but the wife doesn't shit in your garden!'

●

Getting married is like sitting on a toilet seat. It feels good, but you never know who's been there before yer!

●

'Is that you, Chubby?'
    'Yeh!'
'Could you lend me thirty quid?'
'Hang on it's a bad line.'
The operator said, 'I can hear, sir!',
I said, 'Well you lend him thirty quid then!'

●

The old sea captain was deaf. He had no buccaneers.

●

We stopped at the Waldorf. It was just a bit of ground that was walled off!

●

As kids we had those stick-on soles. We had no shoes. Just the stick-on soles!

●

She's so houseproud she puts a toilet roll in the cuckoo clock!

•

She shoves all the muck under the carpet. Do you know, it's up hill to the telly!

•

It was a Orphans Breakfast. Snap, crackle and no pop!

•

Darling, will you kiss me under the mistletoe? Dear, I wouldn't kiss you under fucking chloroform!

•

This watch I bought lasts a lifetime. When the main spring goes it slashes your wrist!

•

Now listen stupid! Now don't call me listen!

●

Would winning the pools change you? Why should it, I've never worked yet!

●

When she lifted her skirt it looked like a bite out of a doughnut!

●

Arthur Scargill was knocked down yesterday. Only a miner accident!

●

Our son was born at an awkward time. He ruined our honeymoon!

●

Irish Rock and Roll singer: shake my balls and rattle my nerves!

●

This fella pulled a razor on us. I wasn't worried, it wasn't plugged in!

●

He said: 'I do bird impressions.' I said: 'I'm not impressed.' So he flew off the handle!

●

I think I was drunk 'cos on the way home people kept standing on me fingers!

●

I took our lass some flowers. She said: 'I suppose I'll have to open me legs for those.' I said, 'Don't say we have no vase!'

●

Didn't have any tea yesterday. The wife burnt the salad!

•

We sold our house this week. The council is going mad!

•

Two cannibals talking. One said: 'She's nice, dad.' Dad said, 'Yes, let's take her home and eat your mother!'

•

He believed in reincarnation. When he died he left everything to himself!

•

There was a mouse in our breadbin. We shut it and let it starve to death!

•

How did you get that hairstyle? Did you put your finger in a light socket? Or did you go through the car wash on your bike?

•

You could get a part in the musical *Hair*. You could be Dan Druff.

•

Is me dinner warm, love?
It is if the bin's on fire!

•

Applause is like food to a comic's ears. Thanks for the tea-cake!

•

The wife's mother came off her motorbike – on the wall of death!

•

Her skin is like a peach. Have you ever seen the skin on a 25-year-old peach?

•

She said: 'That's not my baby.' I said: 'Make your mind up. You told me to change it before you went out!'

•

I got fourteen presents for me birthday. Seven pairs of socks!

•

She was such a bad cook the oven door had ulcers!

•

I met a girl when I was fishing. I don't know whether I caught owt. But I will in a couple of days!

•

She thought a Zulu was the toilet at Flamingo Park!

•

Do you know, I split my wage packet down the middle? She gets the packet. I get the money!

•

She is having a bit of stomach trouble. She can't get her knickers over it!

•

She treats me like dirt. She hides me under the bed!

•

At the airport: 'Carry your bag, sir?' 'No, she can walk!'

•

At the bar: 'Mine's a light.' 'Well, throw a bucket of cold water over it!'

•

He's been married six times. He's not sex mad, just likes wedding cake!

•

It's only puppy love 'cos she licks me behind me ears and sniffs me arse!

•

He might not be a doctor, but you should see him operate!

•

The beer was so flat you could have served it in an envelope!

•

The anti-terrorist squad have surrounded our house. They must have thought our lass was a gorilla!

•

I've bought me wife a Jaguar for Christmas. I hope it rips her to pieces!

•

'Guess how old I am and you can sleep with me.'
    'Hundred and six.'
    'Near enough!'

•

I'm so lazy lately, I won't get out of the bath for a piss!

•

Unemployment, it's so bad! I'm thirty-six and I've taken a paper round!

•

'Excuse me, can I use your Dictaphone?'
'No, you can use your finger like everyone else!'

•

Me mother-in-law has only three weeks to live. I'm not worried – it will soon pass!

•

Scottish fella invited me round to his house for a cup of coffee. From his machine!

•

She's sixteen, our lass. She's having a baby, but she'll get compensation. It was an accident at work!

•

I was born on a doorstep. That's why I've got a lotta bottle!

•

Do you know, I have half a mind to join our club committee. Well, after all, you only need half a mind to get on the committee!

•

He's a maniokleptic. He walks into shops backwards and leaves things!

•

'Excuse me, sir, can I try tnose trousers on in the window?'
 'If you do you'll get me the sack!'

•

Well, ladies and gentlemen, I'll finish off the spot with a tube of Valderma!

•

Dad, why is our mam out all night?
 Shut up son and finish your caviar!

•

The Mother Superior said, 'Come on girls, take those candles out.' She was sick of it wick in wick out.

•

Do you know, she wouldn't hurt a fly unless it had a willie hanging out of it?

•

They are naming a new brassiere after Middlesbrough football club. Plenty of support but no cups!

•

We always go on holiday in the winter. It's easier to get a deck chair!

•

A Scotsman found a crutch and went home and broke his legs!

•

There's a new perfume called Nothing. So, if you want to be the life and soul of the party, walk in wearing nothing!

•

My girlfriend's a bit like a wardrobe. She's tall with drawers.

•

Are those your tits or are you smuggling coconuts into the club?

•

'Would you like to sit down?' 'No, I'll stand for the moment. I've just come back off me honeymoon!'

●

I've had this suit since it was a pair of gloves!

●

She made Crêpe Suzette with crepe bandages!

●

This is a hit song. When I sing it people hit me!

●

This song is so old it was recorded by gas!

●

The Six Million Dollar Man has put a one-armed bandit up the stick!

●

Two divers have just discovered something ten times harder than a diamond.
   They're calling it a British Rail pork pie!

●

The swimming baths were so crowded I dived in three times and never hit the water.

●

This is a business suit. It's a funny suit. Well, it's a funny business!

●

Last night I worked with a Chinese comic, On Too Long!

●

The Irish are launching a new ship today, as soon as they can get it out of the bottle!

●

She might be a blind prostitute, but you've got to hand it to her!

●

She was so thick she had to take her brassiere off to count to two!

●

Heard in a nudist camp:
  Is that Dick Brown over there?
  Yes, we've had a lovely summer!

●

He's an Irish queer. Pat on the back!

•

She said: 'I've had burglars?' I said: 'How did they get in?'
She said: 'I kept a small jar of Vaseline beside the bed!'

•

Paddy was only wearing one glove. He was listening to the
weather forecast and it said it will be cold but on the other
hand it will be warm.

•

Was Noah's wife Joan of Arc?

•

She had a tattoo on her chest. It said: 'In case of rape this
way up!'

•

I called the waiter across. I said: 'Listen Across, this
chicken's cold.' He said: 'It should be it's been dead for
weeks!'

•

We have that many kids that our lass has had to have her
ears pierced so the kids can watch the telly!

•

I joined the Army 'cos I needed the money to buy me self
out!

•

For all the good these suppositories are I might as well
stick them up me arse!

•

The wife has three endowment policies on me so you
could say I was well endowed!

•

I know you were expecting Bob Monkhouse, ladies and gentlemen, but don't worry we've got the club surrounded by snipers!

•

She said she was only thirteen. I said I wasn't superstitious!

•

I've got good news for all the women round here. My marriage is on the rocks!

•

She was as much use as a clothes brush in a nudist camp!

•

Our marriage didn't last long, because her family were getting all the cake!

•

I watched her getting ready for bed. Max Factor, Nivea, mud pack: it was all slapped on. I said; 'Are you ready, Swamp!'

•

I bought her something with diamonds in yesterday. A pack of cards!

•

I bought her a yellow dress to match her teeth!

•

She was sleeping like a baby. She had her big toe in her mouth!

•

I love tall girls. They lie longer in bed!

•

The wife got a Yankee up yesterday. She's seeing him again tomorrow!

•

My mate, he's as tight as a duck's arse. Turns his windscreen wipers off when he goes under a bridge!

•

And he turns the gas off when he's turning the bacon over!

•

Hello, what brings you here? The bus!

•

Football results:
  Motherwell 1 Fatherpoorly 2
  Real Madrid 3 Pretend Madrid 4
  Ajax 1 Fairy Liquid 0!

•

The wife goes to keep-fat classes actually!

•

Idi Amin has a new microwave oven. It seats twelve!

•

Are your ears already pierced or am I boring them!

•

North Ormesby Library has closed down. Somebody stole the book!

•

You mean you're blind and you go sky-diving? How do you know when you get to the floor? I can hear me dog screaming!

•

I've just pinned a photograph of the mother-in-law on the gate. It keeps the dogs out of the garden!

●

You will have seen my mother-in-law before. Her face is on every pirate's flag!

●

She's bed-ridden, but not all the time. Sometimes she likes it on the carpet!

●

I said: 'What do you think of me act?' He said: 'Take my advice, make sure your passport's up to date!'

●

Excuse me, how do you get to the Albert Hall? Practice, practice!

●

I see the Badminton horse trials are a wash out this year. They can't find enough horses to play badminton!

●

Here's an advertisement: Man with kite wishes to meet lady with wind!

●

I'm a diver. My names Muff. I'm a muff diver!

●

A six-foot prisoner and a five-foot prisoner have escaped from prison today. Police are looking high and low for them!

●

Middlesbrough's manager broke into a fag machine. He's looking for ten players!

She always sings when she gets into the bath. You can hear her every January, July or August!

This van is absolutely flawless. There's no floor!

Two crocodiles were on the telly having their leg over on one of those wildlife programmes. My young one said: 'What they doing, dad?' I said: 'Making a handbag!'

If you see more than two Irish men together, they'll be starting an army!

•

Do you know I was eight years old before I found out my name wasn't Jesus Christ.

Every time I came home with my mucky shoes on our dad would say: 'Jesus Christ!'

•

I've just got rid of ten pounds of ugly fat, I divorced the wife!

•

When you're on a diet you think your ears can smell food!

•

If you are ever caught by the cannibals argue with them. Cannibals never eat anything that doesn't agree with them!

•

The kids called her Doorbell 'cos she had no knockers!

•

Do you know the bags under her eyes had handles?

•

When she burnt her bra it was quite a let-down. The lads used to call her the Hunch Front of Notre-Dame!

•

I took her for a game of golf. She got a hole in one, and a sly feel in the other!

•

I love playing darts with her. Well, her head goes to a point!

•

I worked in a Karate school. The wages were poor but I got plenty of backhanders!

•

Like the watch? Got it on tick!

•

This watch cost a fortune, but it's great trying to get the balls into Mickey Mouse's ears!

•

Is that watch gold? It better be or the bloke's done me out of a quid!

•

Yes, I know the tongue comes from an animal's mouth and I know the egg comes from the chicken's arse, but there's no need for all the fuss over Cock-a-Leekie soup.

•

This Japanese drummer, every Christmas he would attack Pearl Bailey!

•

There's an old wives' tale; red sky at night is a shepherd's delight. It's a load of crap. Red sky at night means their fucking barns on fire!

●

Why tell your children about the birds and bees? You want to keep your eye on the bloody rabbits!

●

Woman to the butcher: 'Three pork chops, please, and can I have Irish ones? They're a lot thicker!'

●

A mate of mine paid two thousand pounds out for a sex operation. It left him without a sausage!

●

I'd have loved to been born when I was fifteen years old, then I could have gone straight to work!

●

This feller was so greedy he got married in his back yard so the chickens could have the rice!

●

I should have been at the mother-in-law's funeral today. Still, business before pleasure!

●

My little boy said: 'Our cats just barked like our dog. I put petrol over it and set it alight and it went wooff.'

●

I've never slept with a puff, but I did sleep with a bloke who had.

●

He was a tightrope walker. One night he was tight and the rope wasn't!

●

The concert chairman has booked the Red Arrows, but they can't find anywhere to park!

●

I said to the wife: 'The clocks go back next week.' She said: 'You should have kept up the payment!'

●

Some of these jokes are such crap they'd make rhubarb grow!

●

I said: 'Mam, were do I come from?' She said: 'The sugar bowl, son.'
  I said: 'Dad, I asked mam were I come from and she said the sugar bowl.' He said: 'That's about the bloody size of it!'

●

I've invented a new bath tub. It's only got four sides. You have to put your own bottom in it!

●

Every time I look at her face it reminds me I don't like scrambled eggs!

●

Her chest was so flat you could play billiards on it!

●

She was that thin, when she sat on the back of me motorbike she looked like the aerial!

●

I saw an ice-cream van yesterday. It said: 'Stop me and buy one.' I saw a Durex machine. It said: 'Buy me and stop one.'

●

We used to call her Okie Cokie, 'cos she pushed it in, pulled it out and shook it all about!

●

A dead fly won't hurt you, but forty thousand come to your funeral!

●

We were so poor the Red Cross sent *us* parcels!

●

We used to sell pegs and balloons to the gypsies!

●

This Irishman knackered his football coupon. His cross was the wrong way round!

●

She's about as useless as a log on an electric fire!

●

She was such a good swimmer, she was a street walker in Venice!

●

I'll let you sleep with our lass for your season ticket. Piss off, the season's half over!

●

This is a draughty kitchen. Well, it's breeze block!

●

Kiss me dear and I'll get you a diamond. She kissed me twice so I bought her a Double Diamond!

●

Sign in shop window: 'Ears pierced, while "u" wait'.

●

How much did you pay for that bra?
  Six quid.
  I'd have held them up for less than that!

●

This is a monologue: I said to my girlfriend one evening as
                  we strolled along:
                  They tell me love is a pain in the
                  arse:
                  In that case we're doing it wrong!

●

There was a little girl on the bus. I said: 'You've got a hair on your sweetie, dear.' She said: 'I know and I'm only fourteen!'

●

She'll never vote. She couldn't care less who gets in!

●

What a good salesman he was. He could have sold a double bed to the Pope!

●

My fan club broke up yesterday. The bloke died! I wouldn't mind but they were due to have a mass meeting yesterday in a telephone box!

●

There's that many break-ins, every time you close a window you are liable to trap someone's fingers!

●

Some men like big thighs. Some men like small thighs. But I like something in between!

●

She only makes love to me when she is using me for something, like timing an egg!

●

I was going to sing a song called unforgettable, but I've forgotten it!

●

She's got me eating out of her hand. It saves on the washing up!

●

What's that bit on the end of a Durex for? It's to put your foot on when your pulling it off!

●

He's such a liar. He said he was a long-distance lorry driver on Jersey!

●

To get into the dressing room last night I had to put two pence in the slot!

●

I've had eight happy years with my wife. But I've been married twenty!

●

A drink puts lead in your pencil. What's the good of that if you can't write!

●

He's drinking Domestos. Now he's clean round the bend!

●

Three of our hens have stopped laying. I know 'cos I've just ran over the bastards!

●

I asked the doctor if he had any sleeping tablets for the wife. He gave me a hundred yesterday but she's woke up again!

●

I told Grandad that sleeping with a 17-year-old girl could be fatal. He said: 'Well, if she dies, son, she dies!'

●

Seven days at Butlin's with your girlfriend makes one week!

●

We've sacked the topless waitress. She was dipping in the till!

●

Our mam said our dad was the nicest man she had ever met and she would like to meet him again some time!

●

He's so small he hires himself out on Saturdays to stand on top of wedding cakes!

●

A mate of mine died, you know. Yes, he was putting some milk in his tea and the cow sat on him!

●

I said to the wife: 'I'm not going to work, it's foggy.' She said: 'It's not foggy over the road.' I said: 'I'm not going that way, am I.'

●

I took the wife on a cruise last year. She was a bit worried when the gunboats kept cutting the nets!

•

Pat and Mick sat in a cafe. The waitress said: 'You can't eat your own sandwiches in here.' So they swopped!

•

Her arse is that fat she looks like a bag of sea coal on a bike!

•

The wife said: 'When I'm down in the dumps I always get a new hat.' I replied: 'I thought that you got your hats from the dumps!'

•

I was at a queer's party last night. The chap said: 'Bend down and I'll drive you home.'

•

She had no roof in her mouth. When it rained she nearly drowned!

•

How did the Irishman get the money for a dog licence? He sold the dog!

•

There was no smoking allowed. But I wasn't smoking allowed, I was smoking quietly!

•

I love grandma to take me for a piss 'cos her hand shakes!

•

Great cafe I was in last night. Every time I lifted the plate up there was money under it!

•

There was a deaf and dumb fella in the library. I asked him to put some gloves on 'cos he was making too much noise!

•

Five and a half ton of fish was stolen from Tesco's yesterday. The police are looking for a cat with a heavy goods licence!

•

Did you hear about the Irish firing squad. They formed a circle!

●

A chap said to the doctor that since he'd swallowed a piece of wood he'd got bored stiff!

●

'Paddy your feet stink,' she said. He replied: 'I have to put some clean socks on every day. I've got nine pair of socks on now!'

●

A fella said: 'My lad must be doing right in the Army. He's been promoted to a Court Marshal!'

●

Man to German prostitute: 'What's the VAT for, Value Added Tax?
   'No, vear and tear!'

●

He worked in a gold mine and got caught stealing lead off the roof!

●

She was a grape treader, but she got the sack for sitting down on the job!

●

I've been round the shops to find a new arse, but they've all got cracks in them!

●

Paddy broke into the bookmaker's. When the police caught him he was two hundred quid down!

●

Sebastian Coe's sister has loads of supermarkets. You know Tess!

•

Paddy said: 'Is this a one-man bus?' The driver said: 'Yes.' Paddy said: 'Well, I'll wait for the next one. Me mate wants to get on as well.'

•

Soldier to prostitute: 'How much for the pleasure of my company?' She said: 'Five pounds, sir.' He said: 'Company, left turn!'

•

The teacher asked Johnny if he had six sweets and she took three what would she have. Johnny said: 'A broken arm, miss!'

•

He was so tough he had twigs on his chest!

•

He's so small he fell off the kerb yesterday and his parachute never opened! He has a downstairs window cleaning round! His girlfriend is six foot so he had to jack it in!

•

I called at the George and Dragon. This horrible woman came to the door. I said: 'Excuse me, is George in!'

•

Whisky is my mother's favourite drink 'cos it killed me father!

•

He has a war record. It's 'We'll Meet Again' by Vera Lynn!

•

When you come to my party, ring the bell with your elbow. Well, you're not coming empty-handed, are you?

•

I liked her because she has a wart on her nose. I can hang me cap on it!

•

She has that many double chins, she looks like she's looking over the top of a sliced loaf!

•

It's a risky business taking snuff and sennapods. Snuff makes you sneeze and sennapods dare you to!

•

You always know when the mother-in-law is coming round. The dog sulks!

•

Well if it isn't Mr and Mrs Poole and their son Cess! And Mr and Mrs Bates and their son Master Bates!

•

A prostitute went with a faith healer. He put his hand on her fanny and it closed up!

•

I saw a funny thing yesterday. Two queers were fighting over a manhole!

•

I went to a wife-swopping party. I got a goldfish and a balloon for mine.

•

Would you like the bridal suite? No, I'll just hang onto his ears!

•

Do you know I woke up last night to see if I'd lost any sleep!

•

Last night I was at the grand opening of my agent's wallet!

•

I used to work on a whaler you know. They used me for bait.

•

We've been married ten years and I offered to go down the garden and kill a chicken for dinner! She said: 'There's no need to take it out on him, love!'

•

She reminds me of the sea. Not windswept and fancy free. She makes me sick!

•

I see the mother-in-law is at the door. The mice are throwing themselves on the traps!

•

He was such a bad hairdresser that when he shaved me I couldn't drink a glass of water for a month in case I leaked!

•

I don't think dad and mam liked me. They used to say go and play with the polythene bags son!

•

I said: 'Come on take your tights off.' She said: 'What for?' I said: 'You want to paddle in the water, don't you?'

●

I put Red Rum's manure on me cabbages. The next morning they jumped into next-door's garden!

●

Hartlepool Football Ground caught fire today. There was six quid's worth of damage!

●

To help the club out of financial difficulty I sent them a fiver. They sent me three players back!

●

I've bought my son a space suit but he won't go!

●

The teacher used to bang the piano lid up and down on me fingers just to keep me in time with the music!

●

This act got me a standing ovation at the VD clinic!

●

This was a joke about a wedding ring, but I think it's a bit near the knuckle!

●

There were twenty kids in our family. You didn't dare put your tongue out or someone stuck a fork in it!

●

Excuse me, how dare you have the type of face I hate?

●

I said to the wife: 'Listen dear, it's Wednesday. Half-day closing. So shut your mouth!'

•

He stabbed his mate to death with his sock!

•

I used to drown my sorrows in drink, then I learnt to swim!

•

He died you know when he was shot through the finger. Mind you, he was picking his nose at the time!

•

I'm not a lady-killer but I've crippled a few!

•

I dreamt about Bo Derek last night. I was just about to get me leg over and I woke up. I must go to bed an hour earlier tonight.

•

A new-born little lad looked so lovely. He'd got his father's nose. These transplants are great, aren't they?

•

The IRA man arrived in Heaven. He said to God: 'You's got three minutes to get out!'

•

A traffic warden said it was a one-way street. I was only going one way!

•

Do you know she sucked a lemon and the lemon pulled a face!

•

I was born with a glass eye. Me father was a gypsy and he had a crystal ball!

•

Why can I win at cards but I can't win on the horses? Probably 'cos they won't let you shuffle the horses!

•

Ten pounds buys a boat across the Red Sea. No wonder the Jews walked it!

•

She's got a mouth like a torn pocket our lass has.

•

Have you ever watched a camel sucking a humbug? Then you'll recognize the wife.

●

Paddy ordered six whiskeys. The barman said it would cost him a bomb, but Paddy didn't mind, he'd one in his pocket!

●

My dick's made of emery cloth. It's a rough handful!

●

There was no chance of Our Lord being born in Dublin. Where would they find three wise men?

●

I lost my job for being nine million out. I wasn't an engineer, I was a bank manager!

●

He was so mean, this mate of mine, he went next door to gas himself!

●

This pop singer said: 'This song haunts me.' I said: 'It should do 'cos you're murdering it!'

●

How do you stop a fish smelling? Cut its nose off!

●

These matches will have to be British 'cos everyone's a striker!

●

Jesus said: 'I've got three nails here. I wonder if you could put me up for the night!'

●

Just because that coloured feller's got a smile on his face there's no need to call him snigger!

●

I keep seeing big black spiders. I haven't seen the doctor, just big black spiders!

●

I'm so unlucky, Treets melt in my hand!

●

She was so thin they thought her coffin was the ironing board!

●

I dreamt I was in a forest, with a fella who was selling kippers!
When I woke up I had me head inside her knickers!

●

The train now standing at platforms 3, 5 and 7 came in sideways!

●

It's a new Indigo bra, you know. You fasten it at the back and indigo!

●

There's been a man in the ladies' toilets. How do I know? The seat's up!

●

Football players mark you for ninety minutes. Football supporters mark you for life!

●

An airplane crashed into some flats yesterday. Someone left the landing lights on!

•

I always sit at the back of an airplane. They never back into mountains!

•

The bus conductress gave a chap a wank. She told the inspector: 'Look it says in the manual if he can't pay his fare toss him off at the next stop!'

•

Two sheets came out of the washing machine stuck together. They must have been Omo sexuals!

•

These rabbits in the pet-shop window were five pound a piece. I want to know how much are they for a whole one!

•

Popeye's dick will never get rusty. It's always in Olive Oil!

•

Who is this guy who calls out the bingo night after night? Tom Bowla?

•

Heard about the sporting queer? He'd back himself against anybody!

•

I said to her: 'I've one finger up.' She said: 'Why not put two fingers up?' I said: 'You're not trying to tell me it whistles as well does it!'

•

I always pour a bottle of Mackeson into the piss pot. It saves me getting up during the night!

●

Heard about the Durex made out of a frog skin? You get a longer jump!

●

A chap I know had 'I love Nancy' written on his balls. I said: 'That's a funny place to put it.' He said: 'Well, I bought a ball pen!'

●

She asked me if I would like a screw for the door. I said: 'A feel of your tits would do.'

●

I've got a very vicious guard tortoise. If a burglar breaks in I hit him over the head with it.

●

This chap told me his wife was an angel. He's lucky, mine's still alive.

●

This tart kneed me in the face. Mind you I *was* looking up her dress at the time.

●

This new dress will fit the wife like a glove. A fucking oven glove.

●

She had an acute angina, and her tits weren't bad either.

●

I thought the wife enjoyed making love. I've just found out she has asthma.

●

99

Have you got anything on the Virgin Record label? That means you have to put the hole in it yourself.

●

Do you know I once hurt me neck, and I've never looked back since.

●

Paddy was in the Olympic games. He won heading the shot, and came third in catching the javelin.

●

I'm going to change my stage name to Brillo Pad. I'll definitely clean up in showbusiness.

●

I'm making a new film called *Gums*. It's about a shark that sucks you to death.

●

Little Miss Muffin sat on me face and I ended up muffin' Miss Muffin.

●

I see Snow White's opened a soft-drinks factory. Sne is calling it 7-Up. I wonder were she got that idea from.

●

My barber poisoned his wife. He give her arse a nick.

●

Me Auntie had sugar diabetes. Every time she farted she got candy floss in her knickers.

●

We were so poor the dustman delivered us.

●

When we boil a kettle in our house, next door's wallpaper peels off.

•

This Irish Father Christmas had a sack full of Easter eggs.

•

The first test-tube baby said: 'My dad's a wanker.'

•

There's a rumour going round I've got twelve inches. I don't mind, I started it.

•

Yes I'm a Peeping Tom. I was being tommed while you were peeping.

•

I showed her me dick and she said: 'I'm not that type of girl, I'm a size bigger.'

•

We sent dad a cake with a file in it. The prison governor wrote back and said: 'Your father went to the toilet this morning and filed three inches off his arse.'

•

That blow-up doll I bought keeps going down on me. The sex-shop assistant said I should have been charged extra for that.

•

I was married in a place called Chorley by an Army chaplain. You've heard of Chorley Chaplain.

•

I'm hopeless. When I fell off Blackpool Tower I got lost on the way down.

●

Paddy drove his car into the sea to dip his headlamps.

●

The wife hung her bra on the line and a camel made love to it.

●

I'm so unlucky I bought a banana yesterday that was empty.

●

He got a new pair of cufflinks so he got his wrists pierced.

●

Me mam tied sausages round me neck so the dog would play with me.

●

How do you make an Irishman laugh on Sunday? Tell him a joke on Friday.

●

I said to this girl: 'Sit on my lap, dear, and we will talk about the first thing that comes up.'

●

I called her Treasure, 'cos the lads kept asking where I'd dug her up from?

●

I hope it snows this year, it'll make my garden look like everyone else's.

●

Excuse me, can I hire your donkey? Yes, there's a screw under the saddle.

•

At our local hospital they built a new east wing, and then they built a new west wing. The bastard thing flew away.

•

I was sat eating a Shepherd's pie yesterday. This shepherd come over and punched me in the mouth.

•

The foreman said to the docker: 'There's a gold bar missing off this ship, now hand it over or I will take it out of your wages.'

•

Do you know her face was as crumpled as Colombo's mac.

•

I'll do a quick impression of a one-legged horse. Clip.

•

My wife has had more pricks than a dart board.

•

I went to a topless restaurant yesterday. There was no roof on it.

•

Look at the state of this toilet. Dad reckons he's been taking some Epsom Salts, but it looks as if he's been doing somersaults.

•

I've called my young son after my own father. I called him Dad.

•

In hospital the nurse said: 'Here's your bed pan.' I said:
'Don't say you have to do your own frying here.'

●

Are you the regular gravedigger? No, I'm just filling in.

●

I see they have cleared the River Tees up. You can get
salmon in the Tees now. I've seen them floating in the tins.

●

I said to her: 'I slept with your best friend last night.' She
said: 'You must be a lesbian then. Are you?'

●

Chap walked into the sex shop. He said: 'Have you got
something long white and waxy? Well light it, I've come to
turn your electricity off.'

●

How do you know which is the back of a tree and which is
the front? There's always a turd at the back.

●

What do you call a man who is half beast and half human?
Buffalo Bill.

●

Our wedding was really posh, you know. We had a three-
tiered scone.

Grangetown – My Home Town

Grangetown, the place where a TV licence is as rare as rocking-horse shit! It's my home town.

•

There's that much muck and filth and dust. I've come out of our front door tonight, and I could see this red light in the distance – it was the end of me fag!

•

If you see two people walking together, it's because they're handcuffed!

•

Do you know, you daren't pay the rent 'cos the police would want to know where you've got the money from!

•

The drafts are so bad in our house, they blew the locks off the gas meters!

•

The whole of our street were out tonight to see a miracle – somebody drove up in a car that was taxed and tested!

•

I opened the oven door yesterday, and the woman next door was dipping her bread in our gravy!

•

It's rough out there: even the meals-on-wheels van was hijacked yesterday!

•

I was mugged by a nun!

•

A chap said, 'Can I tap you for a fiver?' I said, 'For a fiver you can hit me with a brick!'

•

If you saw a kid in Grangetown with shoes, he was a cissy!

•

I know one boy who cut his brother's ears off, just because he wanted to use his stereo!

•

A chap come out of the phone box. I thought he was going to ask me for 10p. He said: 'Don't go in there, mate. The bastard thing won't flush!'

•

We were so depressed and hungry, mam threw herself out the bedroom window. Good job we lived in a bungalow!

•

When we had company, dad would lash out and buy a toilet roll!

•

We didn't have shoes. We painted our feet black and laced our toes up!

•

The bedroom was so cold, one day I fell out of bed and broke me pyjamas!

•

It was so damp the mice had webbed feet!

●

And dirty, I saw a rat in overalls!

●

I was born on a revolving door. I've been pushed around every since!

●

They fed me on mushy peas for two years. The doctor who examined me said, 'You'll have to stop, or this child will have a fart attack!'

●

I was an awkward kid! Andrew's liver salts made me constipated!

●

Yes, we never had anything. We were so poor, a burglar broke in one night and left us a quid!

●

I said, 'Dad, why hasn't Santa Claus been?' He said, 'He phoned up to apologize. Rudolph's gone to a stag night!'

●

The thinnest man in the world lived next door to us and we used to call him fatty.

●

I was a tough child. On me fifth birthday I was up at court for biting a police dog. We used to play tig with broken bottles!

●

I think I was seven when my parents first ran away from home, but the police brought them back.

●

I opened a box. I said, 'Dad, it's empty.' He said, 'I know, son, it's an Action Man deserter!'

●

We were so poor we didn't even have a lavatory brush. We tied my pet hedgehog on a stick and told him to hold his breath.

If I had a dog half as daft as you I'd have the fucking thing put down!

●

Well, I can die two ways: I can die of boredom by standing here listening to him or syphilis by going home and sleeping with his lass!

●

If you shot yourself in the head, you would miss your brain by three feet!

●

You must be wearing that suit for a bet!

The Wife

Somebody said to me, 'How long have you been married, Chubby?' I said: 'Fifteen years.' 'And do you love your wife still?' I said, 'No, I prefer her to move her arse in and out a bit!'

Yes, married fifteen years. For the life of me, I can't remember breaking two mirrors.

I've just had half an hour on the rug with her. Well, I thought if we got the corners finished we could sell it this week!

We've just had a row. I said, 'I see my wallet's been through the Bermuda Triangle – there's a fiver missing!'

She said: 'That's not my lipstick on your collar.' I said: 'Too bloody right it isn't, you couldn't keep your mouth shut long enough!'

I said: 'What's the matter with your face?' She said: 'I'm homesick.' I said: 'This is your home.' She said: 'I know I'm bloody sick of it!'

She's been to the blood donors but they wouldn't sell her any!

I bought her a hearing aid for her birthday. I asked her what she thought of it. She said: 'Ten to ten dear.'

She's so thick, she thinks we get all that filth on the TV because the aerial faces the steelworks.

I told her: 'When I die I want you to spread my ashes over the carpet at the bingo hall. Then at least I know five times a week you're coming to see me.'

I wouldn't care if she could cook. She made a cottage pie, and the council came round to condemn it.

Have you ever seen anybody try to make chips with Cadbury's Smash?

She thought *Coq au vin* was something you got in the back of a Transit with one of the lads.

She told me she once went out with a footballer, but he'd get halfway through making love to her then want to change ends!

Then she went out with a cricketer. Every time he got up off the job he'd shout: 'How's that?'

Then she went out with an undertaker, but he was only after her body!

She asked me if I fancied getting engaged. I said: 'No, it's like getting a bike at Christmas, when you can't ride it 'til Easter!'

Mind you, I enjoyed carrying her over the threshold, even if I did have to make three trips.

First time I got her knickers off, I had to say: 'Come on, fart and give us a clue.'

Somebody said to me the other day: 'What's the wife getting for Christmas, Chubby?' I said: 'Big and fat!'

She has a drink problem. Her hand shakes. Mind you it's great when she gives you a wank.

And what an unlucky woman she is. She fell over the other day and broke six legs – she was carrying the dog at the time!

She washed the TV last week and the colours ran.

Nobody likes her. She went to a home for battered wives, and they beat her up!

I came home yesterday and I said: 'I've just passed a black cat on the path. That's supposed to be lucky.' She said: 'That bastard is, it's just had your tea!'

She's got the frying pan and put bath salts in. Then she chopped up a mouse. I said: 'What's that?' She said: 'Bubble and squeak!'

She's been helping the milkman this week. It's just 'til the horse gets better!

She said: 'I'm not feeling very well these days. Do you

113

know, everything I eat comes up.' I said: 'Would you mind swallowing my football coupon?'

I told me mam she was a virgin. Me mam said: 'Leave her, son. If she's not good enough for the rest of the lads in the village, she's not good enough for you!'

She was once raped by a union man. How did she know it was a union man? 'Cos he started late, knocked off early and left her to finish it!

I was just looking at a photograph of the wife bent over in the nude. I took it when we were messing about. Looks like a coconut inbetween two tractor tyres!

She took a photo of me in the nude. She said: 'Eh, isn't your willie little?' I didn't dare tell her I had a hard-on!

And she's cut me down to sex once a fortnight. Mind you, I'm lucky: I know a lad she's cut down to once a week!

We stopped in and watched TV. There was a right sexy film on. She was bending over in the back kitchen, and I sneaked up behind her. I gave her the best ten seconds she has ever had, then I punched her right in the mouth. 'What was that for?' She said. I said: 'For not looking round to see who it was.'

I've just been thinking, fifteen years married. If I'd strangled her on my wedding day I'd have been released soon!

At the Doctor's

Anyway, I went for a jog and I was so slow this fucking steam-roller shot past me. I must have passed out because I came round in the hospital and the doctor asked me if the nurse had given me anything. I said, 'No, I got this dose off a tart in Leeds last Saturday night.' He said, 'I'll examine you for two quid.' I said, 'Good, if you find it we'll share it.'

●

The doctor said, 'What's the matter, Chubby?' I said, 'I'm having a bit of stomach trouble.' He said, 'Can't you get your underpants over it?' I told him I'd do the funnies, if he didn't mind. He said, 'Have you had anything to eat?' I said, 'Nothing out of the ordinary. Yesterday I woke up and had six eggs, $\frac{1}{2}$lb of bacon, $\frac{1}{2}$lb of sausage, $\frac{1}{2}$lb of mushrooms, a bit of fried bread, a bit of plain bread, a yoghurt and a packet of crisps. Then I went to work and had a bacon sandwich, a sausage sandwich, mind you I had brown bread, not white bread because it's fattening. About eleven o'clock I had a hamburger, and at twelve I went to the canteen and had soup, dinner and sweet – sweet was apple-pie and custard, dinner was Yorkshire pudding. Then I had a sausage roll. About three o'clock the ice-cream man passed so I had a raspberry with chocolate on the top. About four o'clock I was at home and the wife had made eggs, sausage, bacon, chips and beans. Then I got ready and went to the club and I called into the fish shop and had fish and chips twice and mushy peas. When I got down to the club there was a wedding on so I had a bit of cake, then I called into the Chinese and had some Egg Foo Yung and curry sauce. The doctor said, 'Hang on, drop your trousers. Here's your trouble, you've only one fucking arse.'

●

Doctor, I'm suffering from kleptomania. Well have you taken anything for it!

●

I was at the doctor's yesterday. I said, 'Doctor, every time I sneeze I get a hard on.' He said, 'Have you taken anything for it, Chubby?' I said, 'Aye, pepper.'

●

Fellow said to the doctor, 'Can you help me, doctor? My wife and I have no sex life at all.' Doctor said, 'Why don't you do it like the animals? Most animals have a great sex life – especially cats, they are out all night shagging each other.' The very next day the doctor bumped into the man in the street carrying a bunch of flowers. He said, 'Doctor, I'm going to the hospital to see the wife. I took your advice, and as I was shagging her she fell off the shed roof.'

●

A man said to the doctor, 'I think I've got AIDs.' The doctor said, 'Go home and have some sennapods and a big bowl of prunes, then treat yourself to a big chocolate laxative.' The man said, 'Will that cure it?' The doctor said, 'No, but it will show you what your arse is for.'

●

The man in the hospital bed said, 'Nurse, give me a kiss.' She said, 'Sorry I can't.' He said, 'Come on now, I won't put my tongue in your mouth.' She said, 'No.' He said,

116

'Well let me just feel your tits.' She said, 'No you can't.
I'm not even supposed to be gobbling you.'

●

Excuse me, doctor, but I think I'm invisible. The doctor
said, 'Who said that?'

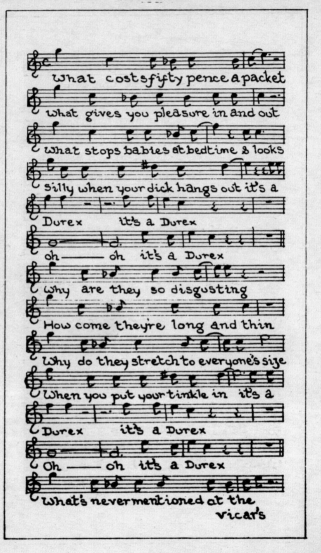

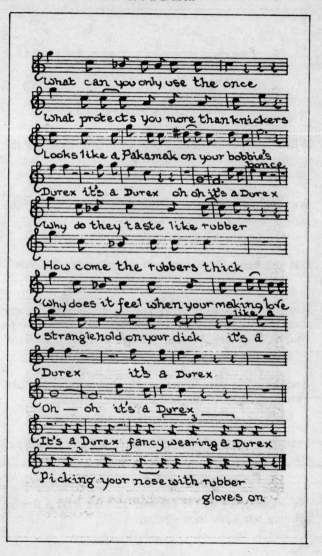

The Weather

When the sun comes out the wife goes pink, so the neighbours call us Pinky and Porky!

•

We took the mother-in-law out in the car yesterday. She kept coming off the roof rack!

•

Did you know the sun was on a Wednesday this year?

•

It was really pouring down last week. One person was shouting, 'I can't swim.' I said, 'The waters only up to your ankles, mate.' He said, 'I'm stood on top of me van!'

•

And wasn't it cold? I snapped a dog off the lampost! Threw some bread out and the birds sat on it.

•

I had two red rosy cheeks on me face. How our lass got her arse on the pillow I'll never know!

•

We go camping in the summer and we start a fire by rubbing our lass's legs together!

•

A bit of hairy fairy on the prairie!

●

We went to Spain and arrived by boat. It really shocked us, 'cos we left by airplane!

●

The pilot said, 'Have you been to Spain before, Chubby?' I said, 'Yes.' He said, 'Is it pear-shaped 'cos I'm lost!'

●

From were I was sat every time the stewardess bent over you could see the cockpit!

●

The wife said, 'If we fly upside down, would we fall out?' I said, 'No, we've been friends for years!'

●

I saw a mouse with a wetsuit on!

●

The flat we stayed in had a rainbow in the passage!

How to Put This Country Back on Its Feet

Save water, piss on a friend!

•

Stop all these smoking experiments with rabbits: find out who's selling them the fags!

•

Have a bit of consideration for the deaf: if you're gonna fart, make it smell!

•

You don't have to get married to be a success. The Pope didn't!

•

Clean the place up a bit, eat a tramp!

•

Let's help traffic wardens and tax inspectors find out who their real mothers are!

•

Never mind about the *Titanic*, let's find out if the iceberg is all right!

•

There's people worse off than us. Look at poor Cyril Smith. Somebody cleans his shoes and he has to take their word for it!

•

Think of my poor father who never had a job. Mind you, he was down as an astronaut, and he wasn't prepared to travel!

●

Keep death off the road, knock the bastards down on the pavement!

●

And when you women are pregnant, swallow a tennis ball so the kid will have something to play with!

Boxing Gags

Twenty-eight professional fights this lad. Lost one, drew two, and chickened out of twenty-five!

•

When I got into the ring women used to scream with delight, because nine times out of ten I'd left me shorts in the locker!

•

I used to box under the name of Rembrandt, 'cos I was always on the canvas!

•

I fought one bloke. I would've had to knock him out to get a draw. He was covered in blood – mine!

•

I was on me back that many times, firms used to fight over the advertising space on the bottoms of me shoes!

•

I boxed one fella and started out really well. I cut him above the head, I cut him above the ear, cut him above the nose – then the ref stopped the fight and took the razor blade off me.

•

Then another bastard hit me so hard I had to pay to get back in. Me corner said, 'Listen, he hasn't laid a glove on you.' I said, 'Well, keep your eye on the ref, 'cos somebody's knocking ten colours of shite out of us!'

●

But I was all heart. I'd hit somebody, then forgive them for falling down.

Dogs

I have a dog – it's an Irish Wolfhound. It walks backwards and waggles its head.

A policeman came to the door. He said, 'Your dog's chasing people in cars.' I said, 'No way – he hasn't got a licence.'

I'll have to get rid of him 'cos his favourite bone is still in me leg.

Every time I shout 'Heel' he bites it.

I had another policeman at the door yesterday. He said, 'It keeps chasing people on bikes.' I said, 'What you worried about? He buries them in my garden!'

Still, you always know when you've had burglars – he hides under the couch!

I help him all I can when he's ill. I bite the postman!

The neighbour said, 'Your dog's pissed on our flowers.' I said, 'All dogs piss on the flowers.' He said, 'Not from the bedroom window, they don't!'

I used to have a dog with no nose. Me mate said, 'How does he smell?' I said, 'Fucking awful!'

I sent him to the paper shop yesterday with five pounds to get me the paper. He didn't come back for an hour, so I went looking for him, and he was on top of another dog. I thought, 'Well, he's never done that before,' and the wife said, 'He's never had the money before!'

We've got a strange dog. We didn't know what it was. Our dad stood on it so it must be a flat-nosed, hissing Bassett.

I think the dog's fallen out with me. He brought me pipe and slippers, then threw them on the fire!

He is so unlucky, when I took him out yesterday a tree pissed on him!

He might have no teeth but he can give you a nasty suck!

He's a one-man dog – he only bites me!

We had burglars one night and he showed them where the money was hidden!

What's the use of having a pointer dog and telling him it's rude to point?

Dog licences are going up – won't affect me, though. Ours is only black and white!

He's no good on the farm, you know. Not only does he worry the sheep, but he knocks on the farmer's door and asks them if they have any mint sauce!

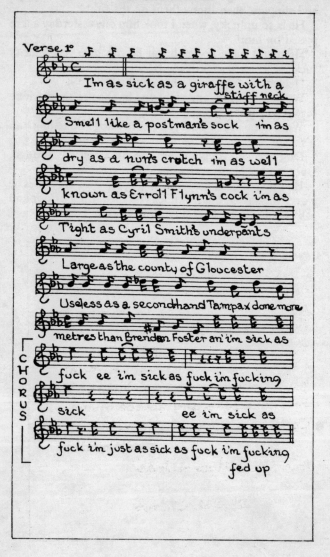

Verse 2°
Thick as a negroes' lips
I'm as wrinkled as John Boy's Granny

I smell like a lavatory brush
I'm about as sore as a honeymooner's

fanny

I'm as lousy as Mick Jagger's vest
I'm as high as Victoria Falls
I'm as hard as a British Rail scone
But i'm as useless as Pope Paul's balls
I'm as sick as

Repeat Chorus

Verse 3°
I'm as friendy as a traffic warden
About as friendly as a rugby team

And i know i've done for comedy
What Kojak did for Brylcream

I've seen more pricks than a

lavatory seat

I'm as welcome as the electric bill
But don't take any notice of me
'Cos i'm a moaning fat cunt

and i'm ill

And i'm still as sick as

Repeat Chorus

Holidays

I'd only been on the plane five minutes and this big fella hovers next to me and says, 'That's my seat.' I said, 'No, it isn't, piss off.' But he insisted: 'It's my seat.' I wasn't moving. 'You're fucking joking, aren't ya?' He said, 'Well, you fly the bastard thing then.'

The next day we went to the beach. This fella comes over to me and says 'Señor, it's sixty pesetas to have a deck chair.' I could have sworn I saw them on sale for eight quid in Woolco.

I'll take England any day. Last year we went to Blackpool. The boarding house was supposed to be three minutes from the sea. It was – by fucking telephone.

We got up next morning and went down for breakfast. The waitress was scratching her bum. I said, 'Have you an itchy arse?' She said, 'Only what's on the menu.' I said to her: 'Is that prawn crackers over there?' She said: 'No, he just likes a fucking good laugh.'

The wife, she's so ungrateful. I got her a holiday in Belfast. All she wants to do is come to the South of France with me.

I once tried to swim the Channel for a cheap holiday. Ten yards from France I got cramp in me ears, so I had to swim back again!

Police

I should have been a policeman. I'm always helping them with their enquiries!

●

I went to prison for something I didn't do: I didn't get to the car fast enough!

●

I stopped one from drowning too, I took me foot off his head!

●

A mate said to me, 'I haven't seen you for six months, Chubby. What have you been doing?' I said: 'Six months!'

●

I would have only got three months, but I was up on a Sunday double time?

●

I borrowed some money off a mate of mine. Mind you, he was asleep at the time.

●

I said to the warden this cells a bit cold. He said, 'Hang on, fatty, I'll ask the governor. He might put you another bar on!'

●

I was in jail for two years. Do you know my wife never looked at another man for days!

●

Copper said: 'Is this your car?' I said: 'Yes.' He said: 'Has Arthur Negus seen it?'

●

I'd been reported for a hit-and-run accident. I said, 'The chap never looked both ways.' He said, 'Why should he? He was stood in his own front room!'

●

I was up at court the other day. The judge said to me, 'You were up in front of me three years ago for the same offence, stealing an overcoat.' I said, 'How long do you think overcoats last?'

●

I was in the car, parked down a dark lane with a young tart the other night and a copper followed us. The copper said: 'Would you mind blowing into this please?' I said: 'Do us a favour, I've just thrown it out!'

I said, 'What is it?' He said, 'It's a bag and it tells you how much you've had to drink.' I said: 'I've got one of them in the house. It's called the wife!'

He said, 'Your back light's off.' I said, 'It's all right, officer. I'll kick it.' He said, 'Well, then, try kicking your windscreen and see if your tax disc comes up.'

He said, 'Didn't you see the arrows on the road?' I said, 'I didn't see the fucking Indians!'

He said, 'I have reason to believe you are drunk?' I said: 'You don't expect me to walk home in this condition do you!'

He said: 'Is this car licenced?' I said: 'Yes, what would you like; brandy, rum, gin or whisky?'

He said: 'Is it automatic?' I said: 'It is but I have to be with it!'

He said, 'Oh, I heard a scream earlier on.' I said, 'Oh, Jesus, the mother-in-law has come off the roof-rack!' 'So it was your mother-in-law that came off the roof-rack?' I said, 'Oh, thank God for that, 'cos I thought I'd gone deaf!'

I said, 'But I've just had the car tuned – it cost me £75.' He said, '£75. Who did it, André Previn?'

When I bought the car the salesman said it did seventy-five to the gallon. I think he meant yards. The car was so old, Stirling Moss's sandwiches were still in the glove compartment.

It's two-tone actually. Black and rust! I'll have to get rid of it 'cos I'm sick of taking me family out for a push on a Sunday!

●

I once bought a Volkswagen, but I couldn't find the engine!

●

I said: 'Listen, officer, I've just done a policemans' ball, and you know what policemans' balls are like. They brought the audience in with blankets over their heads!

●

Two bobbies were talking and one said, 'Listen, you know that young girl that's just got in the police force? I'll be there tonight, right up the fucking piss flap.' The other said, 'Fuck off, ya lying cunt, ya couldn't get your hole in a brothel with a fiver stuck out your fucking ear.' 'Tonight, when you get in our panda car, just tune into my frequency. I'm meeting her about ten to nine.' He picks her up at ten to nine, and he's talking to her, telling her how much he thinks of her and all this fucking shite. They're passing a hot-dog stall, so he gets out of the panda car, goes across, buys a hamburger, gets back into the car, and as he's pulling away he drops it on the floor. She said, 'You're not gonna go down there and eat that, are you?' He said, 'Quick, say a fucking hamburger, quick!'

●

She's a funny cunt our lass. We had a policeman at our house yesterday. He said: 'Chubby, why did you hit your lass with a chair?' I said to the copper: ''Cause I couldn't lift the fucking sideboard.'

●

I was up in court for it. Case before me were bloody funny. Judge says to this queer: 'What's the matter, you are talking very quietly.' He said: 'I've lost me voice.' 'Have you tried sucking a Fisherman's Friend,' said the judge. The queer said: 'Don't you think I'm in enough trouble your honour!'

Our Dad

I take after my father, who incidentally fought with Montgomery in North Africa, and Mountbatten in Burma. He couldn't get on with any bastard, my old feller. Those were the days of rock and roll, it's all cock and dole now, isn't it?

You wouldn't think I was an ugly baby, would you? But I take after me dad. I was such an ugly baby, the midwife slapped our mam. I had that many boils and spots and warts, I woke up in my pram one day and a blind man was reading my face.

I always remember my father saying to me, 'I want you to have all the things in life I never had.' He got me a regular job.

He only ever had one job, my father, and I'll tell you how thick he was: he worked in a bank and got caught pinching a pen. He got everything arse-faced; when he died he left his money to the hospital and his kidneys to me.

My father was a strong union man. When he'd tell us a right good story he'd start by saying, 'Once upon a time and a half.' At one stage he had nine hundred men under him – he used to cut the grass in the cemetery. He had a good line in doughnuts to pygmies for lavatory seats. He always brought me mam flowers home, especially when the park gates weren't locked. He once tunnelled his way out of prison; it took him six months. Very strange, he was only serving three.

Once he was sick on a dog. He said: 'I don't remember eating that!'

He poured whisky on the lawn, so the grass would come up half-cut!

Now he's opened a sex shop on the Falklands. He's selling blow-up sheep!

He sings like a lark: a pillark!

He's so mean he throws confetti on an elastic band!

My father knew what he was talking about, he was down the pits for twenty years. Me mother was fuming – his dinner was still in the oven.

We never forgive me father, you know. Wiped his arse on the will, left us all in the fucking shit.

He had such a large hump on his back, we had to rake the wall out to hang his photo up!

Schools

I was talking to an old school friend yesterday. He said, 'Remember that girl behind the bike shed, she was good wasn't she, but not as good as our lass.' I said, 'Oh, you're right there, she wasn't as good as your lass!'

He said, 'I've ten kids now.' I said, 'Oh, I've only got the one. I used me head.' He said, 'That must have hurt your ears!'

●

Lad next to me in class was always smoking, I set him alight!

●

A girl pissed herself in our class. Teacher said, 'Why didn't you put your hand up?' The girl said: 'I did, but it ran through me fingers, miss!'

●

The teacher said to me one day, 'I think we should have a long talk about girls, Chubby.' I said, 'What do you want to know, sir!'

●

Standing outside the school one day a policeman said: 'You're loitering.' I said, 'I'm not. A fella told me to mind that dog shit and he hasn't come back yet!'

●

I'm like you. I got my sex education at school. They used to think we'd just got off a fucking banana boat at school, didn't they? Used to bring jelly babies in and say: 'This is a little girl, children. This is a little boy 'cause there's a bit more jelly.' First time I took a tart out, I bit her fucking head off.

●

Teacher said, 'Have you fallen out with me, son? You've been bringing me in a big bag of raisins for a full year, and now you've stopped.' I said, 'Oh, me rabbit's dead, miss.'

●

My kid – he's gone to one of them posh schools. I said, 'What's the matter, son?' He said, 'All the fucking kids are calling me "big head".' I said, 'Don't you taking any fucking notice of kids in this street, 'cause they're spiteful. Now go and get two stone of spuds for your mum.' He said, 'How will I carry em?' I said, 'In your fucking cap.'

●

Two old friends, Brian and Ray, bumped into each other on holiday. Brian said, 'My, you're looking prosperous.' 'Well,' Ray said, 'I've opened a business.' 'What kind of a business?' Brian asked. 'I went down to London and I opened a brothel, a three-storey building. Gays on the top floor, paedophiles on the second floor, and lesbians on the ground floor,' Ray replied. 'You must be doing well.' 'I know, but it was hard at first. There was only me, the wife and the kids.'

●

Schoolkids' howlers:

Mary had a little lamb. The doctor shot the shepherd.

●

From a 13-year-old girl's essay: 'I've been to see the Grand Prix. It was very disappointing, it was all about motorcars!'

●

Give me a four-letter word that's used in brothels. Next!

A Trip to the Pub

A man was standing at the bar. A chap came up and said: 'There's a strong smell of cunt in here.' The man said: 'It'll be me, I've been buying the fucking drinks all night.'

•

I went into this pub. Even the piano had a fucking bandage round its leg.

One of my old girlfriends was at the bar and I did a double-take. I said, 'Hello, I never recognized you there with your legs shut.'

She was one of twins, you know. The two girls were stood at the bar and were the double of each other, but I found out one of 'em had VD, and the other one had TB. I made sure I fucked the one that was coughing.

I said, 'Any chance of taking you home?' She said, 'Get me half a lager first.' I said, 'Look, when you go in a shoe shop you always try the shoes, and if they nip you you don't fucking buy them, right? Well I'd like to have a glimpse of the old mot.' She said, 'There ya are, how's that?' I said, 'Fucking hell, that worries me, that. How come you're blonde, yet you're black down there?' She said, 'Well, you know sometimes when you're at home, Roy, and you're putting a picture on the wall, and you've got the nail and the hammer and you miss the nail and you hit yer thumb and it goes black?' I nodded. 'Well, me fanny's had some hammer.'

Any road I took her home, and we were lying completely naked on the couch and her mother walked in.

She said, 'Well, I never.' I said, 'Come on, you fucking must have done.'

She was as common as muck, you'll never guess what she said to me. 'How big is your cock?' I said, 'Three inches.' She said, 'What! A fat fucker like you has only three inches?' I said, 'From the ground, twat.'

I still couldn't satisfy her – that was one hole that could take three shredded wheat.